# SKATING *through* COLLEGE

How to pursue your passions
and make a difference,
without sacrificing your GPA.

## JOHN "IZZY" ISRAEL

ISBN-13 (Print/Paperback) 978-0-9971283-0-7
ISBN-13 (PDF) 978-0-9971283-1-4

Contact John Israel via email at John@SkatingThroughCollege.com,
or visit his website at www.SkatingThroughCollege.com.

Cover and interior book design by Rebecca Feldbush.

## WHAT STUDENTS ARE SAYING:

"I love this book! As a graduate student looking back I needed this book my first four years of college. This book is from a heart of experience and authentic concern. The parts on passion and on academics was straight fire! Something that I struggled with that I had to work out on my own. Would have loved a book like this to help guide me in my early college years."

—Jonathan Salas, student at West Coast Baptist College

"If you're looking for an easy read that provides great practical advice on how to let your passions drive your learning experience in college then you've come to the right place. *Skating Through College* is the type of book you can read, before, during, or even after college to remind you that school shouldn't change your dreams, but teach you how to achieve them. Read the book; I promise your future self will thank you for it."

—Danny Ledezma, student at Pepperdine School of Law

## WHAT PARENTS ARE SAYING:

"As a transformational leader and president of Chicken Soup for the Soul, I always admired John as a college student and role model for my kids. He walks his talk, shows up and is everything a parent could wish for."

—Patty Aubery, parent

"This is an enjoyable read. It's good for students and adults alike. I found myself taking notes on things to work on and to remember. Every graduating senior and their parents should read it too!"

—Jeanne Tanner, parent

"I found this book to be entirely relatable. I love the real world examples from the author and other students. Perfect for a high school graduation gift."

—Cathy Sabo, parent

"As a mother of a college-bound child, I found the wisdom in this book particularly encouraging. With all the new found freedom that college brings, this book spotlights some of the pitfalls John Israel encountered and what he did to get out of that pit and stay out. I liked the personal and unapologetic writing style used by Israel. He speaks to todays generation. *Skating Through College* is real, and the information that can be pulled from it and used immediately is a gift. It's not so much 'how to do' but 'how to think' that will change what you do for the better. This is easily one of the best purchases I will have ever made for graduating students."

—Paulette Britton, parent

## WHAT THOUGHT LEADERS ARE SAYING

"*Skating Through College* is a terrific book every student should read. John Israel's stories and examples cut to the core of the college experience. Whether you are an engineering, sociology, or pre-med major, this book will help you have a LEVEL 10 college experience."

—Hal Elrod, best selling author of *The Miracle Morning*

"Boom! I love this book. John "Izzy" Israel got it right! Each page contains the fuel for achieving your fullest potential and the roadmap to make it happen."

—John Vroman, founder of the Front Row Foundation

# Contents

# Introduction

When you read the title of this book, it might seem like I want people to scrape by, doing the bare minimum. But my intentions behind that title are far from it.

Everyone has a thing. Some people swim, some people play video games. I skateboard.

Skateboarding isn't a hobby. It's life. It's my passion and I was fortunate enough to pursue that passion through out high school, into college and beyond.

It wasn't easy. It was painful physically and emotionally. I was constantly fighting back fear, doubt, and the opinions of others. It was all worth it. I lived my dream in college, which created a different person than the one that showed up orientation weekend. A better person.

"Skating Through College" is a metaphor for success. It's about discovering what you love and pursuing it with your whole heart. Embracing the imperfection that is the college experience. It's about being anything but normal and developing relationships with people just crazy enough to believe in you and support you in the journey. It's about you. The hero.

But why did I write this book?

I wrote this book with one person in mind... YOU! A human being on this planet who actually wants to do something significant with their life, and maybe needs a little guidance. This is NOT a cheesy motivational book where I'm going to tell you to "Reach for the Stars," or "Dream Big." I deal in reality.

Here's how you should think of me. I'm your big brother. The one who made it out of the "post high school" jungle alive with scars and bruises and epic stories to share.

I've made my mistakes. In fact, you will get to read about many of them in this book. You'll probably laugh; you might even cry. At the very least, you'll finish each chapter with some insights, tips, and ideas that helped me to have an extraordinary college experience.

## FIRST THINGS FIRST

This book is designed to be read in whatever order you'd like. Straight through, or you can pick out the topics you are most interested in and just read those. You can knock it out before school, when you're waiting for someone, before you go to bed, maybe even in the bathroom. Yeah, I said that.

I know, I know... You have so much to read and study already. You're a student; you can't possibly handle more.

Well, here's lesson #1: To live a life most people can't, you must do what most people won't. DON'T BE AVERAGE! Leave the excuses for the lame people. You're not lame. You know how I know that? Because you've already started reading this book. You've already surpassed the majority of people who buy books or receive one as a gift and never even open it.

This book will challenge you. There will be exercises and requests that, if you take them on, will help you create amazing stories that are worth remembering not regretting. I invite you to play full out as you read.

For your benefit, I write like I talk. So, don't show this book to your English teacher. She might not like me. I write like this because it's easier to digest. Big words and fancy grammar were not my college major. If it's yours... I'm sorry. I hope we can still be friends.

But seriously, I think the best way to get through to people is to be genuine and authentic. That's who I am, and you should consider aiming for the same.

This book is broken into six sections.

**Part One: My story.** This will give you better insight into who I am and how I pursued my passion while enduring the trials of #1 getting into college, #2 making it through the chaos of college, and #3 graduating with a sense of fulfillment and preparedness for the next step.

**Part Two: The purpose of college.** We dive deep into what most students think college is for, compared to what professors think college is for. The answers may surprise you. This section is designed to give you proper expectations on how to make the most out of the next several years of your life.

**Part Three: Passion.** Ever wondered what your true calling is? Or do you know your true calling but are just unsure how to achieve it? This section is for you. You'll hear stories of both students and graduates who discovered and pursued their passions in college. We'll then dive into the how's of building a supportive network that will keep you on track and open up doors for future opportunities.

**Part Four: Academics.** If I said this journey would be easy I'd be lying. You still have to go to class. Living a full college life and performing well academically is a major cause of stress amongst students. In this section we will reveal time management strategies of elite students so you can get more done with out feeling like you're missing out on the fun stuff. You'll also learn how to communicate and connect with professors to win them to your side in case you ever need to call in a favor.

**Part Five: The difference that makes the difference.** In this section we unfold the one thing that will turn your college experience from good to great. If you're anything like me, you probably want to change the world. Difficult, yes—impossible, no. It's not always about what you get but what you give. Here we look at how to do something that matters, create a movement, and make an impact that lives on even when you are well past graduation day.

**Part Six: The end of my journey.** This is where you get to see the "how it all comes together." All the hard work, late nights, big wins, and epic failures have to lead somewhere. It's how my story ends, and where another begins.

I highly recommend that you write your thoughts down. Either make notes and highlight the crap out of this book, or use a journal as you read, or both. Jim Rohn has said, "Journaling is a great way to untangle the thoughts of our mind." Journaling relieves pressure on the brain from remembering things and it's where our greatest ideas can be captured so they're not forgotten.

Okay... That's it for me. This introduction has been nice. It's great to meet you. Now let's get to work. Turn the page!

# PART ONE
# My Story

# CHAPTER 1

# Skating Through High School

B efore I skated through college, I had to skate my way through high school.

Growing up in a small town just outside of San Diego, California, there just wasn't much to do.

My family didn't have a lot money when I was growing up but my parents did their best. Dad worked for the phone company and traveled a lot. On some occasions he'd be gone for six months at a time. This left my mom in charge and she had her hands full with five kids. I was the youngest.

We drove my mom crazy while dad was out of town. She could have had a frequent flyer card for emergency room visits because someone was always getting hurt.

Sadly, people in our community spread rumors. Many of them judged us and even worse, they judged my mom for how she raised us. She did her best, but it was hard for people to see that. I grew up angry and embarrassed a lot of the time.

I desperately wanted to find a way out of my small town. Skateboarding was my outlet.

There's a stigma about skaters being punks who cause trouble, break things, and have a general lack of concern for their own or other's safety. I am here to tell you that all those stereotypes are absolutely true... Well, not for everyone, but they were for my friends and me.

All that changed when I was 15 after three consecutive, unfortunate events.

**Event #1:** I broke my ankle skateboarding and was forced off my board for a few months. Up to that point I hadn't spent more than a few days without skating.

**Event #2:** Shortly after that, my best friend Geoff was arrested for something that I easily could have been a part of, but I wasn't with him because I had broken my ankle. Nothing short of luck on my part.

This event caused a chain reaction. My parents tried to keep me out of trouble, and they bribed me by saying "If you play at least one sport every year of high school, we'll help you pay for a car." With a car I could go anywhere I wanted, so I was in.

I thought, *What's the easiest sport I can do? Cross country. They let anyone do that. It might even help strengthen my ankle, and it's nearly impossible to get kicked off the team.* "Nearly" is the key word there.

**Event #3:** The final straw to break this rogue camel's back was when grades came out after the first two months of my sophomore year in high school. I had achieved a whopping 1.9 GPA... 1/10th of a point below academic eligibility.

My coach confronted me before practice and said, "You're better than this. I know you are. You just need to prove it to yourself. Until then, don't bother showing up for practice."

I was off the team.

Those words echoed in my head all day. I wanted to argue, I wanted to be angry, but he was right.

They say people change their lives from either inspiration or desperation. For me, it was the latter.

The day I was booted off the team, all I could think about was my family and all the hard work and sacrifices my parents had made to raise me and my four older siblings. I also thought about all those people who had judged me growing up, labeling me as a "troubled teen who wouldn't amount to much."

Coach was right. Before I could prove myself worthy to others, I needed to prove it to myself. I made two decisions that day that changed my life forever.

**Decision #1: Go Pro.** Skateboarding as a profession doesn't pay that well. The one's who make the most have the big name sponsors like Nike, Mountain Dew, or GoPro. If I was going to go for it, I'd need the backing of some pretty big companies to support me. Until this moment I hadn't taken skateboarding that seriously. I was done fooling around. It was time to take things to the next level.

**Decision #2: Go to College.** Realizing that very few professional skateboarders make it past 25 (35 is considered old), I knew I needed a back up plan. No one wants to prepare for the worst, but my recent ankle injury had me think twice. My oldest sister had recently graduated college and found a high paying job she wouldn't have been offered with out a degree. If I wanted a chance to have a better life for my family and myself, I saw college as the answer.

I had a problem. Zero companies were interested in sponsoring me because I wasn't that good, and I had dug myself into a deep hole with every teacher whose class I was failing.

I needed help.

Realizing how responsible I was for creating the situation I was in, the only place to begin was with an apology. That next morning I went to my coach and every teacher and apologized for my attitude and behavior. I wasn't apologizing so I could get out of trouble, I was genuinely sorry and wanted to change.

It was amazing to see how these people, whom I thought hated me, became my biggest fans. We worked together to get my grades up from a 1.9 to a 3.3 in two months, and it never went below that for the rest of my high school career.

I started to set goals for skateboarding too, like picking up my first sponsors. Soon a local skate shop added me to their team and started giving me one free skateboard a month because they saw promise in my ability.

Then I started making bigger goals for myself, like getting a 4.0 and going to the California state championships in cross-country. (Come on, I still wanted that car.) Both of which happened!

Long story short, I got into college. By the time I graduated high school, two more skateboarding companies were sending me free product to support me in my dream.

There my college story begins. As much as I wanted or expected my life to go a certain way, it had a different agenda.

You may never have stepped on a skateboard, but there's probably something that you've really wanted to do with your life.

*Skating Through College* is not about taking the easy route... It's about the relentless pursuit of your dreams.

Before you assume that my college experience was perfect, let me share with you some of the breakdowns and breakthroughs I had. It's valuable to hear about other people's struggles because when you encounter them yourself you can take confidence knowing that you're not alone.

# CHAPTER 2

# Skating Through College

## *Do You Like Roller Coasters?*

---

School, as well as life, can be best described as a roller coaster. It's exhilarating and terrifying at the same time. During my junior year of high school, I came home to find my parents awkwardly standing in the living room. It was as if they were waiting for me to come home, which they were.

They sat me down on the couch and broke the news that my dad had been diagnosed with Parkinson's disease. I didn't even know what that was, but I broke down crying.

They explained to me that Parkinson's doesn't kill you, but it does make life harder. It's what Michael J. Fox and Muhammed Ali have. It's a disease where the neurons in your brain lose the ability to control the muscles of the body.

Some people shake, some people lose their voice; it's different for everyone.

What it meant for my family at that moment was that we needed to come together to support my dad and help out when need be.

My dad was offered early retirement from his 25-year career installing telecommunication systems. He started out as one of those guys who climbs the telephone poles, and worked his way up to the team that traveled the world to install communication systems on U.S. military bases.

The company gave him a severance package and a much smaller percentage of his income than if he had continued to work another 5-10 years, which was his original plan.

We were all a little worried.

And then there I was, getting ready for college. How could I abandon my parents to deal with this alone? How could I subject them to the financial strain of sending me away to school?

That next year was a challenging one for my family. Not physically, but mentally. My dad experienced no physical changes, but we all knew they were coming. To my surprise, my parents encouraged me to go to college anyway and said they would find a way to support me. They knew how hard I had worked to get where I was; they really wanted to see me succeed at the highest level.

I moved up to Washington to attend Gonzaga University. The transition was tough. I spent a lot of time thinking about my family and wondering if I'd made the right decision. There are a lot of great schools in Southern California. I could have stayed closer to home. But I had a mission, and my parents supported me.

Skateboarding in Eastern Washington is not as popular as it is in most other parts of the country. I was a bit of an outlier in my University. There were also so many "Johns" that people had to find a way to distinguish me, and thus my nickname was born. Everyone called me "Skate John."

I was such an oddity on campus that they even wrote an article about me in the school newspaper.

Before I continue, let me explain what the life of a professional or semi-professional skateboarder entails.

This is also true for surfing, biking, and most any other action sport.

Skate companies want three things:

1.  **Exposure**— Companies want people who can skate well and represent their brand while out at the skateparks around future consumers.

2.  **Evidence**— Photos and video. Companies need these promotional tools on their websites, in their catalogs, and for advertisements.

3. **Events**— Contests and demos. Placing or ranking high in a contest is a great way to prove your value. Demos take place in parking lots or at stadiums where hundreds of kids gather to watch their favorite skaters do what they do best. Both of these often require travel.

The last two are really the only ways a company can tell you are still actively skating. If you go more than two months without sending new footage or photos, sponsors will happily cut you from the team. And since there are always young, hungry skaters out there, those who already have sponsorship need to stay active to keep from being replaced.

The difference between a professional and a semi-professional (aka amateur) skateboarder is this: pros get paid to do crazy stunts; amateurs do not. That is, unless they put your photo in a magazine or catalog. But otherwise, amateurs are only paid in free product.

It's just as demanding as any college sport, minus the off season.

## ALMOST LOSING IT ALL

As I was getting used to college life, my major sponsor called to ask how I was handling the transition. I thought things were going fine, but he did not.

After begging and pleading didn't work, I learned my first business skill: *always negotiate with the other's interest in mind.*

Although I wasn't producing as much video footage or as many photos as they would like, I was doing something that hadn't been done before. I was getting a degree. I told the team manager, "Think about the promotional opportunity. Parents are the ones buying the product for their kids. It will make a difference to them to know that one of your skaters is going to college. Do you know how many skaters don't even have a high school diploma? This is great PR for the company." (This is a sad fact, but 90 percent of my pro-skater friends had only a GED.)

"I'm in a city where you guys have hardly any representation, and I'm one of the only skaters on campus. Think of all the students who get to see me wearing *your* clothes and *your* shoes. I guarantee, if you give me some more time, I'll help get more of *your* product in all the skate shops and stores in the city.

After hearing my appeal, the team manager agreed to keep me on and adjusted the expectation of photos and videos I sent them to accommodate for my school schedule. I honored my promise and did everything I could to make sure their product started making it into shops throughout the city.

School life and skate life were going well... Or so I thought.

## ROCKS IN THE ROAD

Little pebbles cause some of the worst injuries on a skateboard. You can see this around campus. Someone rides a skateboard at full speed until they hit the littlest of pebbles on the ground, a pebble they didn't even see, and the next thing you know, BAM! Concrete belly flop.

Midway through my freshman year I hit that pebble in my life.

My mom called, and I could tell from the tone of her voice that this wasn't a conversation she wanted to have.

My parents had done some number crunching, and they realized they weren't going to be able to pay for my college tuition. If I wanted to keep going to school, I'd have to help out.

I'd need to make $5,000 before the start of the next school year to be exact. To some that might not seem like a lot, but considering I had $150 in my bank account from leftover graduation money, and no notable work experience to speak of, I was worried.

That summer after my freshman year, I pounded the pavement and filled out every application I could get my hands on. Unfortunately, because I had no real work experience, I couldn't get a single interview. Until one day a mysterious letter showed up in the mail.

## STAYING ON THE CUTTING EDGE

The mysterious letter touted a "Summer Work for Students Opportunity" and "$16/Base pay."

I immediately scheduled an interview and went in the same day, studded out in the one suit and tie I owned. I hadn't worn these since high school graduation.

The company was Vector Marketing. The Job was selling Cutco knives.

I was interviewed with a group of nine other people. While filling out my application, I noticed that one of the assistant managers was a young guy named Joe from my high school. I immediately connected with him and practically begged him to put in a good word with the manager. Joe said he'd see what he could do.

The manager's name was Paul. He intimidated the hell out of me. At one point, he even kicked out the kid sitting next to me for not paying attention. What was this? Interview Survivor style? After that I shut my mouth and tried not to make a fool of myself.

Once the group interview was done, we filled out a questionnaire, and then had a final interview where they gave us a decision. After pleading with him for a job, Paul hired me. He must have seen how determined I was. Or desperate. Probably desperate.

Either way, I had a job.

Now, Cutco is not one of those weird pyramid schemes. It's a sales job. They have a base pay to take the pressure off the reps, but also a commission determined by how much you sell.

Like most sales jobs, your initial sales prospects consist of people you know because they are more forgiving if you mess up and they are the most likely to give referrals for potential customers.

I was still a little skeptical because there are a lot of scams out there, but I figured if my friend Joe from high school was doing it, I should at least give it a shot.

They started me off at $16 for every presentation and 10 percent commission on everything I sold. My friend Joe said not to worry about the base pay because if I did it right, I'd make a lot more on the sales end. With periodic commission increases based on performance, the best sales reps made 50 percent commission. Joe was one of them.

He let me shadow him for a day after my first week, and I watched Joe make sale after sale after sale. He finished over $2,000 in sales for the day. Ahem... at 50% commission. That means... yep... Joe made $1,000 in eight hours of work, right before my eyes. I was sold on selling.

That summer was the best experience of my life so far. In the next two-and-a-half months I sold $20,000 worth of Cutco and made $5,000. It was more than any of my friends had made that summer, but more importantly, it was enough to pay for school.

## THE PRICE OF FUN

My sophomore year of college was a breeze compared to freshman year. I knew where everything was on campus and had developed a core group of friends.

That is, until one month into the semester. We'd gone to party at a neighboring dorm, only to get kicked out by the resident assistants (RAs) before 9PM. Tails between our legs, we all trekked back to our friend's second-floor suite in Dooley Hall, to finish what we'd started.

As 11PM approached, more people started showing up. Some started hanging out on the outside balcony. Minutes later, our friend Katie rushed in shouting, "Call 911, call 911. Suzie fell. Suzie fell!"

Confused, I ran out on the balcony. Fifteen feet below me, our friend Suzie lay face down on the concrete. She had slipped over the hand railing while trying to win a spitting contest. I've never had a buzz wear off so fast in my life. I flew down the stairs and was the first responder. Suzie, was alive and breathing, but couldn't speak and blood pooled around her head.

Helping Suzie was one thing. Handling all the drunk and frightened students was another.

I took off my shirt and put it on the wound. Then I directed the panicking people as best I could remember from hospital dramas I had seen on TV. I called Suzie's name multiple times, but she was unresponsive. At this point all we could do was wait for the ambulance.

Students poured out from their rooms, and the RAs surrounded us, speechless.

The paramedics arrived, briefly taking Suzie's vitals, and carried her away. All that was left from the experience was the shirt my sponsors had recently given me, now covered in Suzie's blood. I'll never forget that scene.

Next thing I knew, we were questioned by the police. Since Suzie had actually been drinking elsewhere before the accident, we would not be held liable. Not that anyone felt better about it.

No one slept all night. Six AM rolled around, and we headed to the hospital to get an update on Suzie. As we sat in the waiting room, I felt the need to call my dad.

He answered, and I broke down in tears for the first time since the incident occurred. We were all still in shock.

That day Suzie fell into a coma, only to wake up six months later with permanent brain damage, complete blindness in one eye, and partial paralysis on the one side of her body. She'd never return to school.

Those months were significant in my college experience because it was a time when I started making some decisions about how I lived my life.

The next semester, I took a first responder class to make sure that, if I were ever faced with a similar situation, I'd know what to do.

Unfortunately, some things you just can't prepare for.

## OPPORTUNITIES IN DISGUISE

During the second semester of my sophomore year, I received another call from my mom, much like the one I'd received freshman year, but this one more serious.

**Mom:** John, I have to tell you something. I know last year you worked hard and helped pay your way through school, and we're very proud of you. But I'm sorry to say, we just can't do it anymore.

**Me:** What do you mean?

**Mom:** John, since your dad isn't working, all that extra money he was given when he retired is gone. In fact, we're going to have to start renting rooms out of the house just to pay the mortgage. You'll have a room this summer for free, but after that sweetheart, I'm sorry to say, *you're on your own.*

**Me:** (Silence)

**Mom:** "Are you there?"

**Me:** "Yes..."

I won't go into the rest of that conversation because honestly, I'm not proud of what came out of my mouth. I was disappointed and angry. WHAT?... *I'm only 19, and you want me to pay for tuition, food, rent, gas, everything... On my own?!*

## ON MY OWN, BUT NOT ALONE

Every person experiences a moment like this in their lives. For most people, it occurs after they graduate college, when they move out on their own or get a job. It's the moment they become an adult.

"You're on your own!"

Once the shock and anger subsided, I did the only thing I knew to do, the thing that got me through high school when things were looking bleak. I asked for help. I asked my roommate, my girlfriend, my advisor, shoot even my RA. My RA, Nash Calihan, was by far the coolest, most genuinely caring person I'd ever met.

Nash and I had a conversation one day about what I was going through, about how I needed to find a way to pay for my upcoming junior year.

**Nash:** John, have you ever considered being an RA?

**Me:** Not really. Why?

**Nash:** I don't know if you're aware but they give us free room and board for the year, and a stipend of a few hundred bucks to spend every semester. It adds up to about eight thousand dollars in support for the year.

**Me:** (stunned) That would be amazing! How do I do that?

**Nash:** For starters, you definitely don't want to do it just for the money. In fact, don't tell anyone that's the reason you're doing it. There's an application process, and I can put in a personal recommendation for you.

**Me:** Are you serious? Nash, that would be amazing.

Over the next month, Nash did everything he could (ethically) to prepare me. The interview process was grueling, and uncomfortable. In the end, I made it. I actually took Nash's spot; he got promoted and became my resident director (RD).

One of the RD's on the interview committee said, "The reason we are accepting you is because you showed that you can handle yourself under pressure and you respond well to adversity. Suzie's incident was tragic, and you were the first to respond. You followed that up with taking a first responder course. We hope you don't have to use those skills again this next year, but we are happy to add you to our staff, and we know our students will be in good hands."

I was nearly in tears.

# SEEK LEADERSHIP IN EVERYTHING

As amazing as this news was, I was still about $10,000 short of what I needed to pay for that next year of college.

Coming home, I had a lot of distractions waiting for me. Friends wanted me to skate every day, play video games, and go to parties. I really needed to master prioritizing. It was a lesson I learned from first responder class.

If you see someone lying on the ground with a broken arm and they're not breathing, what do you do first? Fix their arm, or get them breathing? You don't have to take the class and be CPR certified to realize it doesn't help to fix a broken arm if the person you're helping isn't alive to use it.

At that time in my life, the only thing that mattered was making the remaining $10,000 I needed to pay for college. Skateboarding would have to be fit into the gaps.

That summer after my sophomore year, I came home more eager to make money than I had been the previous summer. I sat down with the new Cutco manager running the San Diego district. His name was Blair.

Blair helped me create a plan for how much I would need to sell to make $10,000. It was possible.

Interestingly enough, Blair knew about my performance over the previous summer, and also invited me to work part time in the office. He'd give me a small commission off the office, and in exchange, I'd help train some of the newbies, just like my fried Joe had helped me the previous summer. My job was to let people shadow me while I worked with customers every day.

That summer I trained more than 20 people in the field and sold enough Cutco to make a combined $15,000 from my personal sales and office pay—$5,000 above my goal. It was one of the most rewarding summers of my life.

## A YEAR IN LEADERSHIP

My junior year flew by. Being an RA doesn't mean that you just sit back and relax. We had several duties, including:

1. Plan and organize events

2. Go on rounds and make sure students weren't doing anything stupid like holding full-scale Fight Clubs in the basement of the dorm. (It happened.)

3. Make myself available to the students in my hall when they needed help

   ... as well as many other time-consuming tasks.

Take that and add a full load of classes, studying, and skateboarding. My social life was a distant fifth or sixth on the list.

It was hard, but it was rewarding. What I learned about leadership is that it wasn't just a title that allowed me to make or enforce the rules. It required building trust, especially because most students looked at my new role as that of a narc, a cop, and a fun-ruiner extraordinaire. It was ironic, considering how many times I'd run from the cops on my skateboard.

The most important thing I learned from being an RA boiled down to one word— *influence*. I started to realize that when I talked people listened— students and faculty. When you're in a leadership role, people take you more seriously because they know you are making sacrifices every day for the benefit of others. It felt great to impact my community of students. I appreciated the respect it earned me.

The next thing I knew, the two semesters were over, and I had options.

## WHAT'S NEXT?

I'm going to pause my story here, at the summer before my senior year of college.

Let's move onto a more important topic. Namely, *you*.

Why college, why you, why now?

# PART TWO

# The Purpose of College

# CHAPTER 3

# College on Purpose

*How to Graduate and Fail at the Same Time*

D id you know it's possible to graduate from college and fail at the same time? You want to know how?

Don't grow. Don't change.

In fact, do everything the same. Hang out with the same people at the same spots, have the same conversations, and eat the same foods. Don't risk being uncomfortable, and don't risk trying something new. Don't explore the opportunities at your fingertips. Just stay small.

## WHAT IS THE PURPOSE OF COLLEGE?

Have you really thought about your answer?

There are a lot of myths out there about the purpose of college. It's not every day you spend thousands, tens of thousands, or hundreds of thousands of dollars and commit years of your life to something. Especially not at 18, 19, or 20 years old, or whatever age you decide to go to college. So if you're going to spend the money and the time, you should be pretty darn clear why you're doing it.

Approximately 21 million students will enter college this year, and according to the National Center for Education Statistics, only 59 percent of those will graduate with their degree within six years. Um, hello? Anyone else see a problem with this?[1]

---

1 http://nces.ed.gov/fastfacts/display.asp?id=372
http://nces.ed.gov/fastfacts/display.asp?id=40

Why do so many people start something so important, invest all their hard-earned money (or their parents'), or go into debt, and not complete it?

Why do most people give up on things they start? Is it because it's hard? Hard is a relative term; it means different things to different people.

One of the major reasons people leave college is because they started it without the proper expectations or understanding of why they were going.

Imagine that a friend invites you to a party at her house on Saturday. You show up, and everyone's wearing a costume, except you. Your friend notices and says, "Oh, yeah it was a costume party. Forgot to mention that. Well, have fun."

After awkwardly realizing that you are not prepared for this kind of party, you walk around, say your hellos, and if you're like most people, you sheepishly find an excuse to go home. That would be completely normal.

College is just like that party. If you don't have the right expectations going into it, you just might find an excuse to leave the party early. But it doesn't have to be like that.

My belief is that we set ourselves up for failure if we don't start equipping ourselves for success.

I loved college! It was an amazing experience. Many people will tell you the same thing. Some will tell you the opposite. You're reading this book because you are going to college, considering going to college, or you're helping someone in college, and you want strategies for making the most of it.

You're a grown up now. Like it or not, believe it or not, you get to choose how you live your life.

Remember, college isn't *the* answer, it's a place to find answers.

## BELIEFS ABOUT COLLEGE

If you asked an average college student what the *purpose* of going to college is and then asked a college administrator or professor about the *purpose* of college, you'd get two very different answers.

Common Student beliefs about the purpose of college:
1. Experience freedom
2. Get a good job after graduation
3. Find love / hook up (you get the idea)

Common Teacher beliefs about the purpose of college:
1. Develop critical thinking
2. Grow in civic duty and social responsibility
3. Team work[2]

Pretty different, right? Both groups have validity to their beliefs. All of those things can happen in college. But will they? That's the million dollar question.

## THE TRUE PURPOSE OF COLLEGE

If you asked me to sum up the purpose of college, I could give it to you in one word:

# *EQUIP*

The purpose of college is to *equip* you to win in the real world, both professionally and personally.

EQUIP. That's the key. That's why we go to college, isn't it? We feel it will give us an advantage that we might otherwise miss out on if we didn't attend. The truth is that there are thousands of people who never go to college but are better equipped to succeed than a lot of college graduates. Does that mean that going to college is not worth it? Of course not.

The average college grad makes $2.3 million over their lifetime compared to $1.3 million for someone who only has a high school diploma. That's 84 percent more income for college grads.

Does that mean you are guaranteed to make that much more? Of course not. But you have a far greater chance. All it really

2   http://chronicle.com/article/What-Is-College-For-/138683/

means is that you need to bring intention to your college experience so that you are prepared for a better future.

No one wakes up one day and says "I want to be average." No one says "I want to struggle. I want to hate my job."

No one says these things, but they do happen frequently. Why?

Because people miss opportunities in their everyday lives to make little decisions that give them that little advantage.

Every day of college is an opportunity to do that. It's an opportunity to make little decisions that, when compounded over time, will equip you for a better future.

---

*"The things that are easy TO DO*
*are also easy NOT TO DO."*
*—Jim Rohn*

---

# CHAPTER 4

# The Freedom Conundrum of the Real World

*Adults are just kids who got bigger. Whether they grew up or not is an entirely different conversation.*

---

I always hated when people talked about the Real World, as if that's not where I was living right then.

What I understand now is that the real world is the same world, just with the higher stakes.

I remember watching my nephew playing tee-ball when he was five. Virtually everything was controlled. He'd get three pitches. If he missed all three, then they'd set up a tee for him to hit from. They didn't keep track of outs, so every player had a chance to bat every inning. And last, but not least... they didn't keep score, and everyone got a snow-cone at the end of the game.

What a world, right? Very controlled, very little room for failure. Not a bad thing when you're five, but at 25? Disaster.

As we move further and further away from other people controlling our lives and further into adulthood, we get to decide not only what we want to do, but also what we actually do with our lives.

Every student has that moment when they realize, *I don't have to go to class today. No one's going to call my parents and tell them I slept in.*

And this is the conundrum of freedom... You can do nothing, or you can do everything. Either way, it's your choice.

No one forces you to do anything. If they do, you have the right to walk away. There it is... There's your hall pass... you can walk away from everything right now. You could join the circus as a clown or the bearded woman.

Okay, I apologize if you've always wanted to be a clown or a bearded woman, but stay with me.

With great freedom comes great responsibility.

The day you realize you can do everything or nothing, and you choose to do something in alignment with your goals, is the day you truly understand freedom. You understand the age old wisdom, "If it is to be, it is up to me."

This raises the question... what do *you* want?

What do you care about?

What are you passionate about?

What are you curious about?

How do you want to impact an industry, your community, or the world?

Sometimes these questions hurt our brain, but they also inspire us to no end. If you don't know the answers to these questions now, what are you waiting for? Your answers will give you the clarity to find the right bricks for the path you are paving for yourself.

That's why my belief is that college is for one major purpose: to *equip* you for the future challenges and opportunities that will come up.

Challenges will be ever present in your college experience. How you deal with the imperfections of life and remove yourself from the attachment of how it "should have gone" will play out powerfully in your adult life. How you equip or prepare yourself through education and training will make the difference of what opportunities are open to you, as opposed to other more "qualified" people.

Now this doesn't mean there is no room for fun. It doesn't mean that you should never go to a party or take a crazy risk with your life. In fact, quite the opposite. I think you should take risks and challenge yourself.

However, don't take risks that could harm yourself or others, but do take risks that will build your confidence in that future self you want to become: That good mother or father. That entrepreneur. That happily married person. That attorney or teacher. That future self.

Our success and happiness in life is often directly proportional to the risks we are willing to take. It's how we grow. It's how we differentiate ourselves from the pack, and it's what makes us a marketable asset to the world.

## THE SLIGHT EDGE

If you want to make it in this world, you have to differentiate yourself from everyone else your age. You'll be applying for the same jobs or will wind up in the same industries.

*Why should someone choose you over everyone else?*

This question plagued my mind constantly in college. Here I was spending all this money for the possibility of a better future for myself and my family. But was I guaranteed success?

Of course not! It's obvious that going to college won't make you more successful, but it will increase your chances. That's the whole purpose of the Slight Edge Principle. Jeff Olson wrote a book titled *The Slight Edge: Turning Simple Disciplines Into Massive Success*, and in it he asserts that the trajectory of people's lives is directly related to decisions they made much earlier. It's obvious that the life you're living today isn't a result of what you did today, or even yesterday. It's what you did, months, weeks, and years before that dictates where you are now.

Have you ever thought about that? Looking at your life right now, what would you have done differently to create a better situation for yourself? Now this question isn't designed to make you feel bad and think, "Oh, man. I really screwed up." It's a question to motivate you to realize that, if you want a better future, the decisions you make *today and tomorrow* can create the future you want. Your past doesn't matter.

College, if done right, can be a remarkable launch pad for that future you want.

## THE QUESTION THAT BRINGS PURPOSE TO EVERYTHING IN LIFE

Humans are curious by nature. We want to understand why things happen. We want answers.

A mentor once told me, "The best answer to understanding life is not an answer but rather a question. What can I learn from this?"

Think about it. If you succeed at something and ask yourself this question, you can find ways to duplicate that result over and over. What if you fail and ask yourself this question? Even better. If you learn from every mistake you make, or each time that you didn't win, you are equipping yourself to be bulletproof the next time that situation or opportunity arises.

If you flunk a class or a test and you ask yourself "What can I learn from this grade? What will I learn so that this doesn't happen again?" You can find the answers that will put you back on the right path.

If you ask someone out on a date and you blow it, or maybe you go on a date but everything goes terribly, ask yourself the question, *What can I learn from this?*

*WARNING: If your answer to this question is to create a stereotype about yourself or another person, such as "I'm just no good at dating," or "guys are just jerks," you've missed the point.*

You're a living being, not a history book. If you let your mistakes define you or others, they will.

I know, harsh words, but it's the truth. It's easier to blame someone else or circumstances than it is to ask yourself "What can I learn? What can I take responsibility for in this mess? How can I make sure this doesn't happen again?" Those are courageous questions that successful people ask themselves. It's not normal to own your experience, but I don't think you are reading this book because you want to be normal.

But what about when it's not your fault? What if you are the victim of circumstances. Let's say you are in a car stopped at a red light, and the person behind you isn't paying attention and slams into you. Asking the question, "What can I learn from this?" may not make you feel any better or bring any closure to the situation.

When the situation is truly out of your control, you might ask, "Where is the gift in this experience?" Now, that's a hard question to answer five seconds after something bad happens to you. If something hurtful or damaging happens to you, it's difficult to see a gift. Traumatic things take time to heal and distance to properly assess.

Two individuals, Spencer and Kyle, gave me permission to share their stories of some serious and not uncommon issues that many students deal with.

---

# FINDING MY STRENGTH

### Spencer Dixon

Heading out to college for the first time is akin to receiving an adrenaline shot of freedom. In an instant, your level of responsibility is multiplied exponentially. It is a time of extreme happiness and, in some cases, extreme sadness. I have seen throughout the course of my life that people only truly change in moments of inspiration and desperation. College is a breeding pool for moments such as these. Here is one of those moments.

It was a few months into classes and things were going well. I had my established circle of friends; I was dating a girl down the hall, and I had managed to find a job to help me pay for all the partying. I loved California. Then one Friday it all screeched to a halt. My friend Presley invited me to a bonfire at Moonstone beach and introduced me to Laura. She was on another level. She drove her own truck, was surrounded by friends who adored her, and was always up for fun adventures. I was sold; I had to be hers.

Laura and I ended up hitting it off, and we started dating. Things went really well, and we spent a considerable amount of time together—to the point where I started neglecting my other friends. That is a mistake I see a lot of young people make. During their first real relationship, they drop everything and devote themselves entirely to their significant other, forgetting that it's important to have a life outside of each other. However, some mistakes you need to learn the hard way.

About five months into the relationship, we moved in together. It was never something we officially decided—it sort of just happened. Another two or three months later we got a dog, Ozzy. I'm pretty sure I love dogs more than people, and this pup was smart. He picked up every trick I taught him and would follow me everywhere. Not only were we reaching a whole new level of commitment, but I also had slowly begun to resent her. However, I was too scared to be alone and avoided breaking up with her. At this point I was screwed. Laura was pissed beyond belief seeing how much Oz liked me more than her.

After nonstop fighting over silly things, I ripped the bandage off and broke up with her. A few days went by, and I felt as if I had made the biggest mistake of my life. Going from living with someone every day for months to not seeing or talking to them can be traumatizing. I wrote an apology letter and headed over to Laura's house. She opened the door, and inside some other dude we had met at a party a few weeks ago was sitting at her table. I was infuriated. It had been two days! A week or so went by, and she updated her relationship status to dating this fool and told me she had never loved me.

I did what any other rational college student would do at this point: drink. I woke up around 8AM the next morning scraping chunks of something out of my hair. The entire room smelled of vomit, and my body felt as if I had been hit by a truck. When I realized I was sleeping on a bed full of puke, I immediately jumped up, only to fall down onto the carpet. As I laid on my back looking up, I saw red marks smeared across the wall towards my bed. My hand was throbbing, and I could feel the veins in my head swelling and retracting. My room-mate barged in with some water and Advil to save the day. He kept asking me if I was okay and said not to worry about last night. I had absolutely no idea what he was talking about. The last thing I remembered was chugging a bottle of peppermint schnapps.

Still drunk from the night before, I waddled my way downstairs to try and put together the pieces of a fractured memory. Upon taking a closer look at my right hand, I saw there were scrapes everywhere, and it had swelled to about twice the size of my left hand. Definitely broken...

I had officially reached an all-time low. Apparently, I had blacked out, gotten extremely angry, and wouldn't stop talking about Laura. I started punching the wall. My room-mate saw that I was hurting myself and tried to stop me. After carrying me up to my room, I got angry and punched him, too. I didn't even remember it. This was my moment of des-peration, the spark that lit the flame, and the push I needed to change my life for good.

For a few weeks I felt sorry for myself. Prior to breaking my hand, I would cope with sadness by going to the gym or playing guitar. However, having a broken hand made even the most simple things in life—brushing my teeth for exam-ple—nearly impossible. I was forced to figure out a new way to cope with my problems and was disgusted with myself for letting this happen in the first place. I decided to start applying myself in school. I didn't need my hand in order to read. I declared to the world that my revenge would consist of becoming so successful in life that she would regret not taking me back.

As a child, I thought I was not a strong reader. Every week I would go to a reading tutor in order to catch up with the rest of the class. I carried this chip with me for years until this moment of desperation occurred. I channeled the frustration about the relationship into a fascination about my school subjects.

Example: History had always been my worst subject, but, all of a sudden, I was getting A's on all my exams and homework. I discovered I could be good at history if I applied myself. Getting A's felt incredible, though, and it started to become addicting. What else could I learn if I started applying myself and read the books?

Although, at the time, this experience was one of the saddest and lowest moments in my life, I wouldn't trade it for anything. There have been many times in my life when I wished I had never met Laura, but looking back I could not be more grateful for that night at the bonfire. It was an experience that taught me countless life lessons. I wouldn't be the Spencer Dixon I am today if I hadn't broken my hand as an immature 18-year-old. The funniest part is that, to people in my life today, I am known as the guy who reads a ton. I wake up every day grateful for those months with Laura, grateful for the struggles I had to overcome, and grateful for the pain I endured that shaped my character for the rest of my life.

---

# PERSEVERANCE

### Kyle Murphy, University of the Pacific

Having graduated with honors from a prestigious Catholic high school had me thinking college would be a breeze. I had academic and football scholarship offers from different universities. I chose none of those things.

I was 18, and I made it through my orientation at the University of Arizona. I decided to quit promptly after that because I was having a little too much fun.

I soon enrolled at San Diego State, and my time there ended promptly thereafter. Apparently they assumed I would show up to class. What a bunch of weirdos.

Truthfully, I just didn't know what I wanted, and I got caught up in the party scene and developed some pretty serious addiction problems. It was ruining my life.

Over the next ten years, I started and stopped college more often than I care to admit. I actually took more W's than I had credits.

I did not have the right philosophy or the right thinking to be successful. I could show up when other people told me to or when I had to be there, but I had yet to learn how to show up for myself.

I finally went to rehab and got the help I needed. In fact, they helped me so much that I decided to get certified and become an addiction counselor.

Today, I run two of my own businesses. I did finish my college education at the University of the Pacific, 12 years after I graduated high school.

Only one thing mattered in the end for me. I did not quit. I failed forward. I would not trade my experience for anything. I have held a job consistently since I was 14 years old, so I knew how to work.

I needed an education coupled with my work experience to become valuable to the marketplace. Today I am someone who improves the lives around me. We live in the greatest place in all of the world, in the greatest time of all history, with the best technology and the most abundant opportunities we have ever known. I took the risk of being a part of that world, and I love it. I wish for you the ability to never quit.

# PART THREE
# Passion

# CHAPTER 5

# What's the Big Idea?

*A single idea*
*the sudden flash of a thought*
*may be worth a million dollars.*
*—Robert Collier*

*An idea that is developed and put into action is more important*
*than an idea that exists only as an idea.*
*—Buddha*

*The more intensely we feel about an idea or a goal,*
*the more assuredly the idea, buried deep in our subconscious,*
*will direct us along the path to its fulfillment.*
*—Earl Nightingale*

When we have an idea, we have a direction. We may not know how to achieve this goal, but it gives us a starting point.

I used to play with puzzles a lot as a kid, as you might have also. What's the first thing you do after dumping all the pieces onto the floor or table? If you're like me, you look at the cover of the box, which shows what the picture is supposed to look like. Then you look for the corner pieces and start putting it together based on the information you have.

What if I just plopped all the puzzle pieces in front of you and never gave you the box to look at? You'd probably get annoyed, frustrated, and eventually find something more entertaining to do.

That's how most people go through life, with no direction and no plan, which leaves them stuck with whatever the next most exciting thing is. That, or they put together the puzzle someone else wants them to build.

If you're unsure about where you want to go, let me ask you some questions to clarify your direction:

What are you good at?

_____

_____

What do other people recognize you for doing well?

_____

_____

What experiences would you like to have before you graduate?

_____

_____

What can you do for extended periods of time and not get bored with?

_____

_____

What have you done that left you feeling completely happy and excited?

_____

_____

What do you admire that other people do really well?

_____

_____

What or whom do you care about?

_____

_____

Here are a few stories from a few individuals who discovered and pursued their passion in college.

# LIVE WITH PASSION

## Carey Smolensky, Loyola University of Chicago

Before I knew which college I would be attending, my aspirations were to become a dentist. At the time, I was music director of my high school radio station, where I hosted my own weekly radio show, just for fun. Initially, it was more of a hobby that quickly turned into a DJ business. I'd perform at birthdays, Bar Mitzvahs, weddings... you name it.

When I entered Loyola University of Chicago, I majored in biology and lived at home, so that I could continue running my DJ business and making money. It didn't occur to me that I could make a career of it. I was just doing what I loved.

As a freshman, I auditioned at the college radio station for an on-air spot. I soon learned that this was unheard of for a freshman. Students would typically intern at the station for years before even thinking about getting their own show, if they were lucky.

I was awarded my own prime time slot! Countless students were studying to go into broadcasting, and here I was doing it as a hobby. It was a passion that I enjoyed. I started with Top 40 then created a talk show called "Comedy Showcase" where I, along with my very own sidekick, rocked the airwaves with a hilarious, old school comedy show. We even had a joke hotline!

As a college student, I constantly challenged myself to make the most of every waking minute. I learned to adapt to change rather than resist it and to go after anything I wanted. If you don't try, you won't succeed, so you might as well try and give it your all. *You will never regret having tried, but you will forever regret never trying.* When I was not studying, I pursued and explored new passions.

I have long since graduated with a Bachelor of Science in Biology, and although I never used my degree, I pursued my passion for entertainment and event production. Now I have a family of companies under Carey Smolensky Productions, hosting corporate and social events locally, nationally, and globally. I love my life, and *I'm grateful for having gone to college because it gave me the platform to foster my gifts and explore what made me truly happy.*

Check us out at *www.CSPworldwide.com.*

---

## FINDING MY CREATIVITY

### Megan Cahill-Assenza, Suffolk County Community College

I learned the value of taking risks by not being afraid to find and fulfill myself and my passions. When I first graduated from high school, I attended a four year college close to home for three semesters. I transferred to Suffolk County

Community College (SCCC) because my love for learning had disappeared. Out of frustration, I uncharacteristically questioned my purpose for going to school. I did what felt right for me, which was to transfer. It was the best decision I have ever made.

My curiosity to explore various classes and the connections I made with my professors inside and outside of the classroom helped me to distinguish between what I liked and what I loved. From the mentoring relationships, especially with my English professors, I could no longer ignore my passion for creative writing and literature. I love to write stories and poems and have ever since I was little, and I enjoy learning from an author's deeper message that he/she conveys. When I expressed my earnest desire to write, my Autobiographical Writing professor replied in an email, "As we would say way back when, you're turned on in a meaningful way, a healthy life-affirming way... Creativity as a life force."

I found that creativity is my life's force because I was not afraid to follow my heart. I was inspired and excited as to what I would continue to discover and gain. I found my natural disposition of being a true leader, holding student leadership positions for clubs and committees that I was passionate about, as well as giving back to my college, inspiring and helping others.

I discovered my passion for making documentary films when two of my professors gave me the opportunity to experiment with this medium to earn honors credit for their non-honors classes. I found it to be another form of writing for me. I gained more of a sense of self by fulfilling my passions. I was receptive to Jon Vroman's (a motivational speaker who gave a talk on campus) philosophy of living college life to the fullest. The way I fulfill my passions in life is by making connections, changes, commitments, contributions, and by creating. I became a more confident leader serving my college and a confident young woman by fulfilling my passions in life this way.

Being engaged inside and outside of the classroom at SCCC enabled me to discover myself by pursuing and fulfilling my passions with excitement and motivation. The connections I made gave me support and confidence to not be afraid to take the steps that I needed to find and fulfill myself and my passions. I *can* become an author. I *can* become a motivational speaker. I *can* become a professor with my Ph.D. I *can* use my talents and strengths to make a difference in this world. I *can* achieve my dreams because I am creatively passionate.

## CAN I REALLY MAKE MONEY PURSUING MY PASSIONS?

That's a great question. Of course you can. Shoot, you can make money doing all sorts of interesting things.

No job is perfect, and no career is without struggle, but if you do your homework now, you could find several opportunities to make great money in whatever career path you choose.

The one thing to remember is that there are many roles that fit inside every career.

I have a friend named Sandy who loves racing Baja trucks— the ones with giant wheels that climb up and down rocky terrain. Because these trucks are prone to breaking, he learned how to fix just about every part of them. In fact, he became so good that people started asking him to fix up their trucks. This led Sandy to designing and innovating the best ways to make certain parts. Eventually, he focused on one part he made extremely well, better than anyone else in the industry.

That one part is actually all he does now, and he is famous for it. As a bonus, he gets to be a part of pretty much any race he wants in the world because everyone knows him and his craftsmanship. Every part is made in his own garage at his home (well, it's a *big* garage), and he sells them all over the world. Needless to say Sandy does pretty well for himself and his family nowadays, even better than some of the famous drivers who use his parts.

A good friend and colleague Peter Bielagus shared with me this story about how to find the true income opportunities with just about any profession.

---

# CALCULATING THE PRICE OF YOUR PASSION
## Peter Bielagus, University of Miami

Ever since first grade, I knew I was going to be a writer. My passion was fueled not only from love of the craft, but also from the endless words of encouragement I received from family and friends. "Follow your dream" and "do what you love".

As I entered college, however, the words of encouragement from friends and family were quickly replaced. "A writer, huh?" they asked with a raised eyebrow. "So, if the whole writer thing doesn't work out, what's plan B?"

For the first time in my life, I had to justify my dream. Now don't get me wrong, I have an incredibly supportive family, wonderful mentors, and great friends. They didn't ask this question out of skepticism for my abilities but out of concern for my long-term well being. What if I became a writer and it didn't work out? They wanted to know I had something to fall back on.

In my travels, I've met many students who get very offended by this question. They view the inquiry as a judgment of their skills and often dismiss the question as nothing more than jealous criticism.

But I realized that the individuals who asked me about being a writer had zero knowledge of the profession of writing. They knew only two kinds of writers: the famous New York Times Bestsellers and the poor, broke writer who hasn't published a thing.

After a bit of research, I realized that there were many levels of writers. There were those who made $25,000 a year, $50,000, $150,000, $400,000 and even a million dollars a year.

- Page 48 -

None of these writers were famous enough to be identified by the average person on the street.

The dreaded *So what's plan B?* question became my inspiration. I researched all the technical aspects of my dream. How long before the average writer gets published? When a first time author gets published, how much do they get for an advance? How much do they make when a book is sold? Can they sell the books themselves? And what other sources of income do writers have outside of their books (speaking, consulting, etc.)?

Being forced to justify my dream with cold hard numbers was a blessing. It gave me the confidence to realize that even if I didn't become a NY Times bestseller with my first book, there were plenty of opportunities for me to live my passion and make an impressive living doing it.

My recommendation for students is to take some time not only to figure out *what* your passion is, but also to drill down to the hard numbers behind it. How much schooling do you need? What does the average person make in your field? Who makes more? How do they do it? How long does it take the average person to break out?

You'll be surprised at what you find.

---

## BONUS BIELAGUS NUGGET

A friend of mine is a high school teacher who makes $250,000 a year. (That's not a typo.) How did he pull this off? He simply did the research and found *another* teacher who made that kind of money. My friend asked the man how, and the man told my friend that he was such a good teacher that other schools hired him as a consultant. So in addition to his high school teaching salary, he also made money teaching teachers.

Another acquaintance of mine makes $100,000 a year as a magician. When he told people he wanted to be a magician, everyone said, "That's not a job." But now he makes more than they do.

And here is the crazy one. A poet friend of mine makes *no money* as a poet, but his passion for poetry was so strong that he started his own landscaping company. He landscapes in the spring, summer, and fall, spending his days connected to nature. When he is on landscaping jobs, he keeps a notebook with him and writes poems during his lunch break. Then all winter, he doesn't work at all. He just writes poetry. My friend pulled this off by calculating how much he could make as a landscaper working only three out of four seasons a year.

—Peter Bielagus

# CHAPTER 6

# Declar-ify Your Passion

*Declare: to announce officially; proclaim.*
*Clarify: to become clear, to free from ambiguity.*

D eclarify is a word I made up. Hey, it's my book, I'll do what I want. The word declarify is a combination of the above words and definitions and I believe is a great starting point to discovering your life's passion as a student.

The word declare is expresses a commitment or decision of a pursuit or ideal. When you "declare" your major, this is what you are doing. The University doesn't ask what topic you would like to "dabble in" or what major you would like to "try out". You declare and then you go through the process.

In that process you will begin to clarify what your strengths are, you'll begin to discover your favorite parts and your least favorite parts. But you must first declare then the clarity will follow.

The reason I used declare vs. try out is because declaring denotes a level of commitment to a process. Being willing to go through the tough stuff. It's easier to quit on something we are "trying out".

To clarify is like the process of taking off the layers of an onion. With each peel comes distinctions, awareness, and a better understanding of reality as you get down to the core of who you are and the topic you are studying.

To declarify is to commit to an inquiry of what you think you want and in the process you discover what you really want.

Let's expand on this.

## THE PROCESS

Arguably the most annoying question people can ask you is, "What do you want to be when you grow up?"

Nick Swardson, one of my favorite comedians, said, "Wouldn't it be a crazy world if we all became the first thing we wanted. There would be ninjas and princesses running around, and quarterbacks throwing footballs to pirates."

Fortunately, we aren't locked into the choices we made when we were six and seven years old. Although... ninja...

The reality is that most people think their path to success is linear, but in fact it looks a little like this.

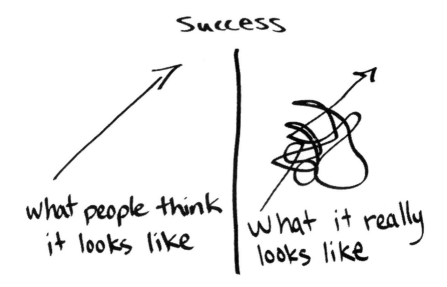

Now those squiggles can mean many different things. They could represent a challenge, a failure, struggles at home with family, a terrible break up, or losing someone close to you that changes your ultimate outlook on life.

Problems are an inevitable part of life. No one is immune to adversity.

*The problem with problems is when*
*you view your problems as problems.*

The point is, often we start going in a certain direction, and one thing leads to another. We wind up in a completely different place than we expected. And that's not always a bad thing.

## UNCOMMON PATH TO SUCCESS

When you enter college, you may not be 100 percent certain of your career path. Test it for yourself. Ask 10 people who are in a career path that you admire, and ask them what their major was in school. Ask around, and you'll likely find about 50 percent whose major is directly related to what they're doing now.

This raises the question, "If there's a good chance I won't use my major, what am I going to college for?" One of the things that employers look at, more than your major or where you went to school, is the fact that you finished something you started. Yep! That's it.

Now engineering, accounting, and medical jobs often require certifications that your major will play a direct role in. However, too many students stress about having the right major, as if their life depends on it, and they miss out on one of the golden opportunities in college.

The golden opportunity in college is to explore your gifts. What are you meant to do?

## MEET B.J.

B.J. Ward is a top real estate broker in Ventura, California. At 27 he was on the cover of the *National Association of Realtors* magazine for his success at such a young age. I sat down with B.J. and asked him about his high school and college life.

He went to the University of California Santa Barbara on a basketball scholarship and had no aspirations to get into real estate.

His dream, like most college athletes, was to make it to the pros. After his third year on the team, it became clear that B.J. was good, but wasn't going to be a member of the select few in the NBA draft.

B.J. remembered an early mentor of his who was very successful. The man volunteered to coach his club basketball teams, yet seemed to have a lot of money. B.J. said, "I didn't know what he actually did. I just knew it was business and I wanted in."

His mentor ran a successful real estate company that B.J. eventually interned with during his senior year at UCSB. Five years and many home sales later, he started his own real estate company, Comfort Real Estate, where he has 10 agents working for him at the time of this writing.

B.J. grew up living in an apartment his whole life and says one of his proudest moments was helping his parents buy their first home only shortly after he bought his.

B.J. is someone I believe "skated through college" in the sense that he pursued his passions on the basketball court as far as he could on a competitive level. That habit to do what he loves has translated into his success in business and life. I have great respect for how he found a way to apply his talents and gifts to the market place and adjust quickly when he found out that basketball wasn't going to go any further. That's a hard thing for many student athletes to accept, but it's a reality for most of us.

He still plays basketball on the weekends, and coaches a youth basketball team. Now he gets to be on the other end of the spectrum inspiring young athletes and essentially doing for others what his mentor did for him.

# WHERE ARE YOU?

Right now you are in one of three places in your life:

1. You have NO idea what it is you want.
2. You have an idea of what you'd like to do, but are open to other options.
3. You absolutely, without a shadow of a doubt, know what you want to do with your life.

Whichever one you are, just know that you are in the perfect place. These aren't the levels from which you can grade yourself as a person. It doesn't matter where you are; it matters that you're moving forward.

It is through action, not meditation, that you will find what you will do next with your life. Notice how I didn't say "you'll find your true calling in life." What you'll discover is that, as you're on the journey, you may get to a certain destination you've been striving for, only to find out it's not all it's cracked up to be. But because you relentlessly pursued your dreams, you saw an opportunity for something greater.

# MEET NATE

Nate was a self-made millionaire who started his success right out of high school. Since he was a little kid, Nate wanted to play professional baseball. At age 17, he was drafted to play for the Houston Astros upon his high school graduation. He was about to start living his dream.

Unfortunately, while playing football with some friends, Nate had a serious injury that would prevent him from ever playing professional baseball. He was crushed. But instead of sulking about the life he could have lived, Nate kept moving forward.

Nate liked to work out, and after high school he took a job as a salesman for an exercise equipment manufacturer. With no experience behind him, Nate did what he did best: studied and mastered the product details until he knew them forward and backward. Within a very short time, Nate caught the attention of the company owners because he was selling more units than anyone in the company.

They asked him to help open a retail location, to which he replied, "Only if I can have 50 percent ownership in the store." After mustering up the money from his personal savings and that of his family, Nate was able to purchase a 50 percent stake in the store. To no one's surprise, Nate made that store more successful than any other in the state.

By the time he was 21, he sold the business, profited over $1 million dollars, and moved onto his next venture.

## WHAT ARE YOU WAITING FOR?

The two biggest beliefs that stagnate young people from finding out what they want to do in life are the following:

1. I have to pick something I'll be passionate about for the next 30 years.
2. I have to know the answer now.

Most people don't take a first step because they are worried it's the wrong one, assuming there's a right one.

*The only wrong decision you can make
is the one you don't commit to.*

There's always an element of risk when doing something you've never done before whether it be in college, on a skateboard, or in life.

In skateboarding, the worst injuries happen from the tricks I tried and bailed on half way through. I'd jump down a set of stairs and kick my board away because I was scared of slamming on the concrete. Interestingly enough, if I kicked my board away I'd almost always slam anyways. I was committed to "trying" the trick, not "landing" it.

Oddly enough, when I committed to landing the trick, I'd still often fall the first couple of times, but I'd have a clearer picture of how I could land it. After a few more tries, I'd usually pull it off.

That's how life works. When you're committed to trying something, but you aren't committed to giving it your all, you hurt yourself.

On the flip side, when you commit, you find a deep-rooted strength inside yourself that can do just about anything.

There's nothing wrong with changing your mind, but do it after you've given it your best.

We're all professional starters. Few of us are professional finishers.

You happen to have read the stories of two individuals who took similar entrepreneurial paths, but for very different reasons.

B.J. enjoyed being a part of a team, liked business, and enjoyed the opportunity to lead (just like he did in basketball). Nate liked the independence of having complete control over his life and business so he can grow it and build it on his own terms.

What's important about goals is not the goal itself. I'll repeat that... *What's important about goals is not the goal itself.* Rather it's that you are in active pursuit of *something*. But what? ANYTHING!

For me it was skateboarding, the challenge of trying new tricks, and doing something no one had ever done. For you it could be art, music, or building things. Maybe you're great at listening to your friends and want to start writing an advice column for your school newspaper. It doesn't mean you have to do it forever.

Explore the opportunities provided by the college landscape.

# CHAPTER 7

# Before You Climb the Ladder, Make Sure It's Leaning Against the Right Building

One of the biggest things that holds people back from taking action on their future careers and life goals is the fear that they will pick the wrong path. Unfortunately, a lot of students use that as an excuse to not do anything. And the only thing worse than picking the wrong thing is picking nothing.

People will often encourage you to pursue real world experiences in fields that you are interested in *before* you fully decide that it is what you want to do. And, the sooner the better.

Now, you have to realize that every job has a component to it that you won't like. That is simply reality. But, would you also agree that everything worth doing has a hard part?

For example, I love going to theme parks with roller coasters, but you know what I hate? Lines. Standing in line for hours on end is one of my least favorite things to do, especially when it's hot out. Anyway, the point is that when you pursue your job or career of choice, you will inevitably encounter things that you don't like about it, but you will also likely find things about the job that you love. And unfortunately, we don't always get to separate the hard parts from the things we love. It's baked into the cake, if you will.

The smartest thing you can do is take the time to meet a mentor in your industry and ask questions. Make sure to read the section on "How to Find a Mentor" to give you some insight how to do that. But, you must also realize that there are some things you have to experience for yourself to understand if that is truly what you want to do.

For the longest time I thought I wanted to be a doctor... until I volunteered at a hospital for a summer. You know what I realized? Most people who come to a hospital were either really happy or really upset. Either someone had a baby, or someone was really hurt—and you can imagine which one was more common.

I recognized that the hospital environment wasn't something I was interested in because it contained more negativity than I wanted to deal with on a daily basis. Now, that doesn't mean it's a bad job. It just wasn't for me. Well, I'm glad I didn't wait until I was through with medical school five years later to figure that out.

One of the greatest things you can do with your life right now is expose yourself to many of the opportunities and people in the industry that you are curious about. Engage with everything you have, and you will find your strengths and weaknesses, likes and dislikes. The sooner you identify these things and begin to build on your strengths and learn to eliminate the things that you despise, the sooner you will find yourself sliding into your ideal career path.

Here is a story from Erik Wilde about what he learned interning in the corporate world.

---

## DISCOVERING WHAT I DIDN'T WANT

### Erik Wilde, University of Southern California

It just wasn't for me.

Not that it's a bad life; many of my friends do this every day and seem to be happy. It started as a summer internship, offered to me by a mentor who was a very successful guy. In fact, he was the president of a division in a Fortune 500 company. He knew me well enough to know that this internship was going to give me a taste of corporate America, and I ate that opportunity up, every last bite! Little did I know it would give me indigestion, heartburn, and the corporate plague, but my mentor did. He offered it as a paying internship to wash it all down.

I remember the first day. I felt on top of the world. He guided me to my cubicle while my coworkers eyed me with disdain and distrust. *Who was this young guy being walked to his cubicle by the President of the company?*

I had no idea how big of a deal that was. So, of course, these coworkers essentially became my boss, and I had to carry the weight of an Olympic lifter, not just because I worked for them but because they resented the fact that the boss-man was handing it to me on a sort of silver platter. I wanted to prove to everyone I was smart and that I belonged there.

The first week was awesome! At 6:00AM my alarm would ring, I would put my suit on, grab my coffee, and head to the office, just like I would be doing for the rest of my life. I proved to my peers at the office that I had a strong work ethic and could handle anything they threw at me, and even started to make friends. Life was good.

Week two came around, and I realized on Monday morning that I wasn't as excited as I had been the first week. I thought, *I'm just a little tired; it will wear off.* I worked all week on my inventory audits and delivered my reports to the managerial staff just as I had in week one, full of pride.

Week three started, and I was sort of dreading going to work. I got to my cubicle that Monday morning with a new stack of inventories to sift through as I prepared my spreadsheet. By mid-week, I was gazing at my reflection in the computer monitor wondering if this was it. *Is this what I'm supposed to be doing with my life?*

I kept reminding myself that I had to start somewhere, and I knew that, if I took opportunities like this and worked my ass off, I would climb that ladder of success. Once I climbed another couple of steps, I would have an office, not a cubicle; I would be dictating the reports I needed to the interns, no longer be the one preparing them; and I would be living the dream! I finished week three with a renewed vigor.

Week four started, and *I couldn't get a smile on my face.* I reminded myself that I was getting paid and had been given an incredible opportunity by my mentor; it was also a resumé builder, so off I went. I walked into my cubicle, and it seemed my stack of inventory papers had doubled. I could feel the bile start to rise. I looked over the top of my cubicle, thinking it was maybe some sort of joke. Were they messing with me? Turns out no; they started me off with a light load, and now I would be performing audits at a normal rate. I about jumped out of the seventh-floor window!

As I sat there that day, observing the corporate office environment with the classic cubicles, the utility room with all the copy machines, and the ever so popular break room, I concluded that this lifestyle wasn't for me. Most of the opportunities for a fresh business graduate from college are in the corporate world, and there is absolutely nothing wrong with it. You can climb that ladder of success and work hard to achieve your goals.

For me, I knew I could never have this day-to-day routine. *I knew I needed to be out there, where the people are.* I needed to be vocally communicating with people and not stuck in a cubicle where I felt confined. It made sense to me as I was then attending the entrepreneurship program in the business school. I needed to be my own boss, where I set my hours, where my work ethic could dictate my success, and my earnings were limitless; *I needed to be an entrepreneur!*

I finished my internship and thanked my mentor profusely for giving me the opportunity. When he asked me if I wanted to seek employment there full-time after graduation, I had to call him to answer as I was running so fast for the front door he wouldn't have been able to hear me. When I eventually called my mentor, I could sense his smile through the phone. He knew I wasn't coming back.

After this experience, I graduated with a degree in business and found there were a plethora of opportunities in the marketplace.

Now, I am an entrepreneur. I have a new set of challenges to deal with daily, but I don't regret it. In fact I don't regret that internship either. Sometimes you've got to learn what you *don't* want to do to discover what you *do* want to do.

---

# TECHNICAL DIFFICULTIES
### Michael Costigan, London School of Economics

I started my first small business, called madFusion, in high school. I formed it with a few of my friends, and we made some money on the side doing marketing, advertising, and web design.

Although it wasn't something that would make the *Wall Street Journal*, it lit a fire inside me. I wanted to be an entrepreneur.

In the summer of 2010, I was nineteen and living at home with my parents. I had graduated high school the year before and made a last-minute decision not to attend any of the colleges that had accepted me across the country. Both my parents (who showed it) and my friends (who hid it better) were worried. Did I really know what I was doing? Would I decide to go to a college with late admission? Travel for the next year? Go work at a fast food joint?

Throughout high school, I had made it clear that I wanted to strike out on my own with both a business and a brand that I could use to generate income and ultimately influence. However, when the time came to choose what was next, I wasn't ready.

The business I considered starting wouldn't support the lifestyle I wanted, nor would I be happy living at home. So, after weighing both sides, I decided to work an entry level job in sales at the Apple Store in Irvine, California. For the next 12 months, I saved and lived at home. I watched all of my friends move away, live in dorms, attend college parties, and travel. It certainly wasn't in my five-year plan to still be living at home. I thought I had made a huge mistake. Maybe I wasn't meant to go down a different path?

As time went on, I thought I had surely wasted a year and would have to return to school, so I decided I needed to do something bold. I used my savings and signed a lease on an apartment I couldn't afford in Los Angeles, two hours away. Most people probably think I had just made a terrible decision, but I saw it as the ultimate motivation. If the fear of being homeless (or worse, returning to my parents' house!) couldn't motivate me, nothing would.

I was working every angle, but without a degree, or a job that met the high median income of the area I was living in, I was running out of options.

Finally, the month that my money would run out rolled around. I was more disappointed in myself than scared. I thought I had failed. And then, one day, I was with a group of friends. We talked about the things we were working on, and I happened to mention something that resonated with one of them. A week later I was asked to lead market development in the area of cloud services at a tech startup—a role similar to what I had done in my startup during high school. Despite my lack of formal qualifications, this person saw my skills and potential to help scale their business. We've since grown the staff six fold, and I'm now the director of strategic development.

As far as college goes, I finished my degree through an external program pursuing my passion. It was the best of both worlds.

Today, I've reached a point where I can pursue my own brand. I travel to speak at colleges and conferences, while also helping to build a meaningful business in the internet security space. Sometimes you don't know if your decisions will lead you to success, but to not take those risks would be to deny yourself the chance of becoming who you truly want to become.

# CHAPTER 8

# Get Comfortable Being Uncomfortable

O nce you accept that the purpose of college is primarily to equip you for the future, then here's a reality: If the future you want is different than how you live now, you'd better get comfortable being uncomfortable.

## BREAK DOWN BEFORE A BREAKTHROUGH

Studying anatomy and physiology was fascinating to me because the human body's ability to heal itself is nothing short of amazing. If you've ever worked out, you know the next day you'll be feeling pain. Our muscles literally rip and tear apart because we force our body to lift a weight heavier than our muscles are used to. It's not used to the stress.

The internal body craves balance and consistency, but it's also intelligent. If you lift weights repeatedly, the body makes note and says, "Well, this is the new environment. Every week this new strain is here. Better build bigger muscles to handle this." And that's how muscles grow... through consistent repeated stress on the body.

The real battle is not as much the physical pain, as it is the emotional pain. The pain of growth feels similar to the pain of injury... yet they are not the same. Of course you can injure yourself lifting weights, but more often than not, the pain we feel is the body's indication that it is under stress from new circumstances. So what do most people do after that first day of working out? You guessed it—they quit or creatively come up with excuses like "I'm busy." It's a natural reaction to being uncomfortable.

But that pain is good. In fact, it's necessary if you want to grow bigger muscles. So the real challenge is to continue to push those muscles incrementally until they are comfortable handling that stress, and the only way they will be able to handle that stress is by growing.

Now, we all know you don't get super fit from one day to the next, or even one week to the next. It takes time. Herein lies the challenge: your physical body is like your internal state, a creature of consistency and habit. To get into shape you not only have to overcome the physical challenge, but also the mental challenge to get yourself back to the gym, day in and day out. It won't feel good; it won't feel right. You may start to make up excuses about your old self being "not so bad. I mean I don't want to be so vain that I'm just trying to look good; I like the way I look. I'm just going to take it easy." Then we go back to the way we've always been.

Realize that your body and mind have a preference for normal and always pull for consistency. If you want to do anything remotely significant with your life, especially something you've never done before, you'd better get comfortable being uncomfortable.

This is why understanding the success trap is so important.

## THE SUCCESS TRAP

If you've made it to college, you've probably worked hard and achieved some level of success to get you there. The challenge now is that what got you there won't get you where you want to go.

We all like to win. If you played any sports and were a hot shot in your school, or maybe you dominated a certain subject like math or English, you probably created an identity of success in your mind. This is important because we love success; we crave it. But (and this is a big but) there is no way you will always be successful and win when you pursue something new.

Sorry to break it to you. This is one of the biggest challenges for students because, as you enter the world, you will have a reality check about your actual skills and abilities. Don't confuse your failure with "maybe this was never meant to be."

Too many students have this issue because some things are easy to come by. We want things, and we want them fast. That mentality is one of the driving forces of innovation and technology, but it is also causes great stress and anxiety in college students. Sustainable success doesn't come easy, and it doesn't come fast.

## THE GARDEN VS THE GROCERY STORE

Have you ever gardened? If you haven't, you at least know how it works. You plant a seed. You water, and you wait. If you want to help your plant along, you might add some fertilizer, but you'd inevitably be looking at a pile of dirt for a while. Then one day, a little sprout will pop up. *Oh joy*, you think, only to wait for another month or two before anything cool shows up. Eventually, the plant matures with fruit and you get to reap the reward for your hard work and patience.

The grocery store on the other hand, works completely differently. You show up, buy what you want, and move on. But how did that food get there? It was planted, grown, and packaged by someone. It took months of production to get to that grocery store. We just show up and consume it.

Now before the grocery store mafia comes after me, I'm not saying that grocery stores are bad. I go to Trader Joe's and Costco all the time. But, it's important to remember that, while we live in a culture where things are easy to buy quickly, the people who make and sell products to you are the ones who make all the money.

Businesses take time, attention, and planning to produce the opportunity to buy what you want. But don't make that assumption about your future.

Good things take time. Do the work. Earn the right. Don't wait for what you want to be handed to you. Be prepared to get your hands dirty and engage. It's fun, and it's worth it.

# REALITY CHECK

I remember being in college and heading to my first major skate competition. It was called the Sound and the Fury, and it was held in Seattle, Washington. I had always placed somewhere in the top three whenever I entered local amateur competitions. But this was the first time I would be competing with people from all over the world, including athletes from such places as Spain, Canada, and Brazil.

I was pretty confident that I'd do well because, you know, I had always done well in these types of competitions.

As soon as I stepped in for warm-up practice, I knew I was in trouble. These guys were good, really good. The best of the best. To add to my nervousness, I'd never skated in front of so many judgmental eyes in my life. Not only did that intimidate me, it psyched me out.

I didn't even place high enough for them to tell me what place I finished in. I was embarrassed and I felt like I had failed.

Two valuable lessons came from this experience:

1. **If I wanted to become a professional, I needed to prepare like a professional.** Wanting something badly doesn't replace the need to practice and prepare. You have to work at it day and night if you want the opportunity to become great at anything.

2. **Always be on the court.** Even though I didn't perform or place how I wanted, something great came from putting myself out there. While at the competition, I made a key connection with the team manager of a skate supply company. That connection turned into a sponsorship for me a few weeks later. That sponsorship added to my credibility and ultimately more sponsorships from other companies. Had I never shown up, had I not risked that momentary failure, I would never have made that connection that opened so many other doors.

## WHAT GOT YOU HERE WON'T GET YOU THERE... OR WILL IT?

So I lied. Sometimes what got you here *will* get you there.

One important thing to remember is that when you look at what you do well now, you probably had to work pretty hard at it before you attained the skills you have today. Can you remember how it was when you first started? Were you as good as you are today? Probably not.

The people who seem most successful at pursuing their passions in college, whether it be sports, business, music, or medicine have to keep themselves hungry for what they want. Have you taken the time to visualize who you want to become? Have you closed your eyes and imagined the emotions you're going to feel when you win, save that life, or look at your bank statement and notice all the commas between the numbers?

Successful students constantly look for best practices and always look to gain advantages when they can. Just because you study hard for a test once, doesn't mean you're going to do well in a class. It's your daily discipline and practices that will separate you from the pack.

Rory Vaden said it best in his book *Take the Stairs*. "You don't own success. It's rented. And rent is due every single day."

So, yes. The landscape has changed. Life is more competitive. That doesn't mean you can't excel at it. You may need to take an honest look at your strengths and what you really need to work on, to take it to the next level.

## DID I _____ TODAY?

Did I write today?

Did I work on my business plan today?

Did I play piano today?

Did I work out today?

Did I ride today?

Did I climb today?

Did I make my art today?

Did I (fill in your passion) today?

Well... did you?

It's a simple question and if you answered yes, congratulations. You are entering into the realm of people who earn the right to do work they love and you'll need to work on it every single day.

As a student you will need to accept that you'll never have enough time. You need to make the time. As you grow older it will not get easier. Life doesn't slow down because you want it to.

My friend and author Peter Voogd says, "You can have reasons or you can have results, but you can't have both."

Did I skate today? That was the question I asked myself constantly.

The weather was pretty harsh the months of November through March where I went to college. Snow and rain make skateboarding outside nearly impossible. So what did I do? I connected with a group of other students and we would get together and go around town finding all the underground or covered places to bring ramps and rails to skate together. It was so cold that we'd deck out in snowboarding clothes just to skate.

On other days I found the indoor racquetball courts that hardly anyone ever went into and I'd skate for about an hour. Was it allowed, probably not, but no one ever said anything and I got my practice in.

Perfect circumstances do not exist. You can wish and hope for the weather to be different, for your class load to be lighter, for your family/friends to be more accepting but it won't get you anywhere.

Did I skate every day? Of course not, but that was a question constantly on my mind and it served me well by refocusing my priorities so I could find time to skate AND do my school work.

I wasn't perfect. Sometimes my grades suffered a little, but then I'd skate less and study more. It's a never-ending balancing act to pursue your passions as a student. Be ready to forgive yourself constantly for making mistakes. Just do your best.

It's about progress, not perfection.

*If you work on your craft daily, magic happens.*
*If you "think" about your craft daily, nothing happens.*

It's simple... go to work. Little by little. Day by day and soon enough your skill level and preparation will become known, first to you, then to the world.

Part of the joy of becoming an expert or a Pro is remembering the amount of time you put in to be where you are. It's called street cred. Earn the right.

# RISK-REPEAT

## Leah Recancia, Saint Mary's College of California

I learned the value of taking risks at the age of 18 when I decided to move away from home and everything I knew to live on campus as a full-time college student. When I attended university, it was almost harder to make friends because the atmosphere is similar to high school in that the students are cliquey, but this time I was the new girl.

Moving away to get my bachelor's degree was a big deal. I took risks to live in an unknown place, meet new people, try new things, and work really hard to make it to the next year of exploring the unknown, meeting more people, and trying newer things. Repeat four times— at the very least.

There is a big difference between *going through life* and *living*. The more you can be purposeful and embrace change, the more you will benefit from life. I didn't realize what I was doing at age 18 or that taking this journey was a huge risk. All I knew was that I had to keep doing it until I got it right.

I tried out to be a cheerleader on the spirit team. I auditioned to be a dance company member. I ran for class vice president. I joined numerous clubs. Now don't get me wrong, I was nervous as heck every time I tried out because you know what happens when you try out... you might not make it. Some things I didn't succeed at; some things I did.

Consequences occur from taking risks, and usually they're found in one of two categories: benefits or trade-offs. While I accomplished many things, I also risked friendships, lost time to study and time to myself, and I eliminated any opportunity to travel abroad. We call these risks the trade-offs. But there were so many more benefits I gained from these risks. I became well-versed in different subjects, which made me better able to relate to different kinds of people.

I also challenged myself to wear many hats, and in doing so I lost and found myself. This kind of risk-taking paves the way to figure out who you are, where your passion really lies, and what you are truly capable of doing. Learning to embrace change and living on purpose comes with time and experience. So experience all that you can and have the courage to always take a risk.

Looking back on my college career, if I can tell anyone in college right now one thing, it would be to not hold back and to not care about what others think.

———————————————

# CHAPTER 9

# Feedback is the Breakfast of Champions

I f you want to make a mark on this planet and do something significant with your life, do this one thing and you will instantly set yourself apart from your peers: Ask for honest feedback from someone qualified to give it.

This is why you hear so many top academic students talk about connecting with their professors. If you want to do something well, ask someone who's already done it or who can show you your blind spots.

You are entering the global marketplace with people who've been doing your job, or pursuing what you want to pursue for years. They've been through it, and you haven't. But that's okay. Remember *things worth doing well, are worth doing poorly at first until you can do them well.*

That's why college is the perfect landscape to explore as many opportunities as you can.

Why do great athletes and teams watch recordings of themselves practicing and playing? They get another angle.

Why do they have coaches? To notice what they themselves couldn't see.

But why do we only utilize this concept inside of sports?

Could a teacher give you feedback?

Could a friend give you feedback?

Could a loved one or family member give you feedback?

Of course.

Here's a story from a student who worked for me for a period of time.

## KEVIN'S STORY

A student named Kevin worked/interned for me while he attended a local community college. Kevin was a bit awkward. He constantly spoke out of turn, accidentally offending people, and in general had a tough time making friends.

He was a reader, so I handed him a book by Jack Canfield and Kent Healey called, *The Success Principles for Teens*. It had some nuggets in there that I thought might help him.

Two days later he came back, and something was different. He started to be aware that his actions had consequences with other people.

He then did one of the bravest things a student has ever done in front of me. He asked for feedback.

He said, "John, I just read a chapter on asking for feedback and realized that I might be doing some things that are hurting more than helping me. Could you give me some feedback so I can change, become a better person, and be more effective at the job? I really like it here, and I want to continue working for you as long as I can."

Wow! I was floored. No one had ever asked me for such unbridled, authentic feedback.

My respect for this young 18-year-old grew ten-fold in ten seconds.

We talked for a good 30 minutes about how he could improve and become more tactful with his communication. Kevin worked for me nearly two years while he was in college, and it was an honor to watch him grow and mature as a young person.

It impacted both of us in such a way that I wanted to share with you six steps to asking for and receiving feedback.

# HOW TO ASK FOR AND RECEIVE FEEDBACK

1. **Ask the right person.** Asking your friends for feedback on how you can become a better student won't get you the same results as asking the teacher whose class you're struggling in.

2. **Ask for honesty (and prepare to hear it).** Tell them, "You won't hurt my feelings. I won't take this personally. I just want honest feedback of how you think I can improve."

3. **Take notes and clarify.** Write down notes about their feedback and read them back to make sure you've understood them correctly. *Important: DO NOT justify or make excuses for past behavior at any point in this conversation.* It will completely torpedo the whole experience.

4. **Do a gut check.** Some of the things you were probably expecting to hear while some may be a new perspective you were hoping for. On occasion someone will give you an opinion that will not necessarily serve you. It's just their opinion. Take the time to look at what you feel is worth working on and what to take with a grain of salt.

5. **Take action.** Are you committed to growing or not? Sometimes we want to justify our actions. Everyone has stuff. Don't assume yours is more important. Get to work on honoring their recommendations.

6. **Follow up.** Check in with the person after a few weeks or months to review your improvement and gain more feedback.

If you have the courage to do something like this you will gain two things:

1. **Improvement.** You WILL get better, if you accept the feedback and make the changes.

2. **A proponent.** A fan in your corner. People you respect have other people who respect them also. Being a person

of influence, I've helped students get into grad schools and connected them with job opportunities. When someone is humble enough to ask for feedback and do something with it, they've earned my respect and my personal stamp of approval.

What's one of the bravest things you can do right now? Find someone you trust and ask them for honest feedback.

# CHAPTER 10

# Who's on *Your* Team?

---

Connections make the world go 'round.

All humans crave connection, and in the relationship game it's quality over quantity all the way.

The late great author and speaker Charlie Jones stated, "We will be the same person in five years that we are today except for two things: the people we meet and the books we read."

College is such a remarkable time and opportunity to meet and experience life in a totally different way than you'll ever expect.

The first friend I ever made on campus was my roommate from freshman year. His name was Brandon. He came from Portland Oregon and was a big ball of energy.

Over the first two months of school, Brandon and I became pretty close. Yes, we had our bouts of "Did you eat my last granola bar?" and "Please don't leave the radio on full blast when you leave for class." Ahem... Okay, I'm over it now. Brandon even invited me to his home for Thanksgiving since my family was so far away. Then something happened.

I came home from classes one night, and I saw Brandon sitting outside of our dorm room with a 40 oz. beer in broad daylight. I thought, *What is going on here?*

**Me:** Um... Hey Brandon. Are you all right man?

**Brandon:** (No Response)

I knew something was up. As I got closer, I saw tears filling his eyes. Eventually he said something I'll never forget.

**Brandon:** My dad just passed away today.

**Me:** What? How?

**Brandon:** Car accident in the middle of the day. He didn't see it coming.

I could hardly believe it. I'd briefly met Brandon's dad when he moved in, and that guy was the life of the party, just like Brandon. He was in his mid-40s, had a great job, and supported four kids as the sole breadwinner.

Brandon succumbed to a pretty severe depression in the days and weeks that followed. This wasn't in the student handbook. I didn't know what to do. So I asked for help.

I went to campus counseling to get advice on how to help Brandon.

The school therapist said, "Make yourself available to him. Try not to force him to talk, but just make sure he knows that you're there for him and when he's ready to talk, you're ready to listen."

Brandon did eventually talk, and I did spend Thanksgiving with his family (three weeks later). The impact on me was no-where near what it was on Brandon, but it drew us closer as friends. Brandon and I were roommates three out of the four years we were in college. We went on road trips together. We double dated. Brandon was even a big help when my dad was going through his own health issues. I became a more grateful person for everything I had because of Brandon.

That's what college is about. It's not about having 2,000 friends; it's about building relationships with people who support each other. It might be scary to lean in when people are going through something, but there will be a time when you need it, too. Build deep relationships with people, and you will build a lifelong network of friends.

# CHAPTER 11

# For the Social Butterfly or the Antisocial Caterpillar

N ow if you are the social butterfly, you may have no problem meeting or getting to know people on campus. That's
awesome. You just might be that person who "saves the
day" for your less-social counterparts. Your challenge may not be
having the guts to talk to someone; it may be having the patience
to listen.

If you're the antisocial caterpillar, this is the time for you to
grow those wings. Now you don't need to stand on a table and
yell, "Hey look at me." That would be weird. The thing for you
to consider is that whatever you fear about meeting other people, they probably have similar thoughts, fears, and insecurities
themselves.

I remember someone telling me, "A stranger is just a friend
you haven't met." It made me reframe my thinking and realize
that people aren't so scary. And the way you make something less
scary is by making it more familiar. The more you know about
something, the less you have to be scared of it. The same with
people. So what's the answer if you're an antisocial caterpillar...
the answer is QUESTIONS.

Learning to ask good questions about the other person actually takes the focus off you. *They* are the ones talking. How great is
that?

Remember this: *Great relationships aren't always about what
you do or say, but how you make people feel*. If you make them
feel awesome when they are around you, then they will love you

being around. We always enjoy spending time with people who make us feel like we matter.

Here are five dos and three don'ts every social butterfly or antisocial caterpillar needs to know to create great friendships/relationships in college.

# DO

1. **DO give others an opportunity to shine.** Involve others in your conversations. If someone's talking, give them your full attention. It's easy to get carried away with your stories because it's fun to tell them. Just remember, the other person likes it too, and when you listen, the person telling the story feels like you actually care about them. Let others talk, too.

2. **DO ask questions.** Be curious about the other person. Not like "Hey, what's your social security number?" but like "Why did you decide to go here? What has you interested in chemistry? What do you love about where you are from?" They might be an excellent musician or a closet metal head. *Everyone is fascinating.* It's your job to find out how.

3. **DO listen with your whole body.** It's important to make sure that when you listen, it's clear that you are *listening to them* with your eyes, ears, and body. Have you noticed when you try to tell your parents something important while they open the mail or they're on the computer, it feels like a waste of time? Consider that other people feel that way when *you* are on your phone while they talk to you. Look them in the eye while they talk. Show facial reaction and expression to what they say. Don't allow yourself to be distracted by things going on in the background. Listen to them as if what they are telling you is

the most important thing in the world. Of course, don't be weird and over-exaggerate your reactions; you might come across as insincere.

4. **DO pay attention to the energy you bring to the conversation.** It's been said that some people brighten up a room when they walk into it, and some brighten it up what they walk out of it. Harsh words, but we all have at least one friend who constantly brings negativity to a conversation, and it's just a bummer. Remember, it's okay to vent if something is bugging you, but check it out first. Ask "Hey, is it cool if I vent for a minute?" Just remember, the goal is to talk about it so you can get over it, not so you can ruin the other person's day.

5. **DO pay attention to time.** There's nothing worse than talking to someone when you KNOW you need to leave for class, or when you're talking to them on the phone and you KNOW you need to start working on homework. Consider other people's time—I can get caught into this trap myself, so I learned to ask, "Do you have a few minutes" before I start unloading my day on them. Or ask, "What are you heading off to next?" This will make sure you BOTH respect each other's time.

# DON'T

1. **DON'T be a one upper.** Have you ever finished telling a story you were really excited about, only to have your friend tell a much cooler story?

   You tell them how your family went to Hawaii for summer break, and they tell you how their parents have a beach house in Hawaii and they go there every summer... and one time they were attacked by a great white shark while they were surfing, but they fought it off with their bare hands. Okay, maybe that's a little extreme, but you get the idea.

If you're like me, you not only felt like what you did wasn't THAT cool, but also you probably started to secretly despise that person. Just a little.

That's called being a one upper. Now, consider that you might do the same thing to others once in a while. When you hear someone telling a story, maybe something similar but MORE exciting happened to you... don't say anything about it.

Don't share your story. And this is *really hard* to do, especially when you have such a great story and you're on the same topic. Let their moment or story be special. It will create a better friendship when they enjoy being around you rather than feeling uncomfortable telling you great stories because you always have something better to say.

Again, relationships are all about how you make the other person feel. It doesn't make you or your story any less significant. It simply means you care more about the relationship than being the center of attention.

2.  **DON'T think of your reply while they are still talking.** Do you ever notice that, when someone is telling you something, you check out and start to think of what you want to say next only to realize you've stopped listening to them? We all do it. But it's frustrating for the other person. You've experienced this. You get this sense that they are just waiting for their turn to talk. It deflates your desire to continue telling your story. Just sit there, listen, and what there is to say will come to you. Trust yourself.

3.  **DON'T finish people's sentences.** This ties in with thinking of a response while the other person is talking. Isn't it frustrating when we're trying to talk and someone keeps interrupting us? It's like, "Hello, I'm an adult. I can finish my own sentences." It makes us feel like a little kid.

Give people the time to finish what they are saying. Everyone thinks and speaks at a different pace. You never know, you might not be correct when you start assuming you know what they are going to say. And all that does is prove you weren't fully listening to them. This one requires patience.

Most of these are common sense, but what's common sense isn't always common practice. Try these out and I bet you'll notice a difference in the relationships you build on campus.

# CHAPTER 12

# The Front Row

All right, here's the nitty gritty of the purpose of this chapter. When you want to do something extraordinary with your life it will often grow and develop with, or be crushed and diminished by, the people in your life. One of the benefits of learning to be social and meeting people is that you will get to find the people who have similar values and goals as you.

The reality is that college is a landscape unlike any other you'll experience in life. It's filled with people just like you, making a transition with hopes of a better future. Now many people, most of them in fact, are still trying to figure out what the hell they want to do with their life. If that's you, that's okay.

Here is a harsh but valuable principle that will transform your college experience.

*Everyone deserves your respect, but not everyone deserves to be in your Front Row.*

## WHO'S IN YOUR FRONT ROW?

My friend Jon Vroman is a world renowned speaker and founder of the Front Row Foundation. They take people with life threatening illnesses and put them in the front row of their favorite event like a concert, baseball game, etc.

Recently Jon posed a question to me. "Who are the top 10 people in the Front Row of your life who get most of your attention RIGHT NOW?"

It's a tricky question because it's really two questions: Who are you spending most of your time with, and who do you want to be spending most of your time with?

Most of our relationships growing up came from proximity. Neighbors, school friends, sports, music, extracurricular activities. We're kind of forced into relationships with people around us, whether we like it or not. I think it becomes a default belief that we don't really choose our friends, they just kind of happen.

But why does the question "Who's in your Front Row" matter in college? Because college is a fresh start. No matter who you were friends with in high school, no matter what your reputation was or wasn't doesn't matter from here on.

A lot of how we know ourselves is based on how others relate to us and what they know about us. It's kind of refreshing when people don't know you or judge you for all your mistakes in the past.

Your Front Row relates to you however you want them to, based on the relationship you create with them RIGHT NOW. You get to be whoever you want in college.

Whether you're staying local or moving away, starting college is like the reset button on your social game console. And for some of you, it'll be like playing a *brand new* game. Which is both exciting and terrifying at the same time.

Our quality of life is directly related to the quality of our relationships. Whether they be friendships or significant others, the people we spend our time with impacts our experience of life.

Remember: *Everyone deserves your respect, but not everyone deserves to be in your Front Row.*

The Front Row are the people who have the greatest influence with you and often, not always, you have that influence with them. They're the ones you're excited to share big news with, but also the ones that you go to for counsel when you're dealing with something difficult. However, they're also the ones that build you up when you need it most, rather than allow you to indulge in your mediocrity.

Here's a litmus test to see if someone truly belongs in your Front Row: *Does being around this person make me want to be a better person?*

Think about it. Do they elevate your standards or bring them down?

Author Matthew Kelly says, "A good relationship is where both parties help each other become the best versions of themselves."

Imagine a life filled with these types of people. What could you accomplish... together?

Not everyone who's in your Front Row this semester will be in your Front Row next semester. That's okay. By intentionally cultivating the relationships you want, you take steps towards having the support that'll help you achieve success. And unlike others, when you reach the mountain top, you won't be alone when you get there. Take a moment and fill in the blanks on these lists.

Top 10 people you spend time with NOW

1. _____
2. _____
3. _____
4. _____
5. _____
6. _____
7. _____
8. _____
9. _____
10. _____

Who do you want your Top 10 to be?

1. _____
2. _____
3. _____
4. _____
5. _____
6. _____
7. _____
8. _____
9. _____
10. _____

Now this doesn't mean that you need to break up with your friends (although some of them...). All it means is that you choose who you spend your time with. In class, you can't always control who sits in front of, next to, or behind you... But you get to choose who you study with.

Remember, relationships are a two-way street: The right relationships aren't just the ones that give you the most. They are the ones where both people support each other the most. It won't be 100 percent equal all the time. There are instances when certain relationships require more energy and time. If the other person is going through something and you are there for them, that favor generally comes back. Life will ebb and flow for you over the next several years (and hopefully decades); supporting those close to you can pay dividends when you need it most.

Here's a great story from graduate Don Anque.

# ACADEMIC SUCCESS STRATEGIES-DATING MATTERS

Don Anque, Syracuse University

My girlfriend and I met at a work party a couple of months before my second year of college. She was two years older than me and the leader of the art club at school. She had already premiered some of her work around Los Angeles and would graduate in the spring.

After leaving the grocery store one day, I drove to my girlfriend's apartment to cook dinner. I unloaded all of the groceries while she was reading for a class in the kitchen. She took school very seriously.

Oftentimes, she would enlighten me with the critique of an artistic movement over the course of a meal. Her friends described her and her work as inspirational and thought-provoking. For many, she was a genius. On one of our dates, there was an extraordinary description that came to my mind after learning about her more—*she was out of my league... and that was a good thing.*

College can be a difficult experience. Finding a major that radiates in harmony with your life goals and GPA expectations is an incredible task if you are continuously facing roadblocks. On top of all that, dating the wrong person can make your problems a lot worse.

College roadblocks may include troubles with understanding the course materials, roommate issues, or other disasters. For many, grades are the number one indicator of collegiate success. In order to achieve success, a number of academic strategies must be employed. Finding someone who pushes you to study harder and develop into a better person all around is an element of academic success that is easily overlooked. There are many opportunities for partying and distractions that pull you away from school. The wrong kind of partner will bend your will toward negative experiences.

The fallout from these negative experiences is that you are not growing, academically or developmentally.

Because of the demands placed on new graduates after college, it is often said that students must treat their classroom experience as preparation for real life. Employers or graduate admission committees will look at your grades and application materials, which reflects the choices you made in your college career. Based on this small sample of you, they will make a determination. They will see connections between your grades and application with your decision-making abilities. For an employer, are you a good fit for the company? Will you help expand the business? Will you be an ambassador for the profession? For an admissions committee, should you be allowed into higher scholarship?

Dating the right kind of person will motivate you to crush every test and destroy your professor's standards of excellence. It's a transformative experience.

# CHAPTER 13

# Befriend a Few, Be Friendly to All

O f course you want to spend as much time as you can with your Front Row, but that's not always an option. You can and should be friendly to everyone because you never know when you'll see them again and impressions matter. Who knows, some day they may work for a company you're interested in.

## MEETING DEAN

Before committing to attend my university, I came up to tour the campus. The guy who showed me around was named Dean. After being shown around, I went back to the dorm where I'd be staying for the weekend. It turned out Dean also lived there. We hung out more that evening and the whole weekend. I had such a great time with Dean and his friends that, before the weekend was over, I decided *this* was the school for me.

Five months later, I saw Dean on campus. He was just the same to me then as he was when I visited. He was genuinely a cool guy, and we remained friends for the next three years before he left for grad school.

Fast forward to three years after I'd graduated, Dean messaged me on Facebook. Apparently he was applying for a job at a major company in Boston, and it turned out that the person interviewing him was a friend of mine from high school. Small world!

Dean asked if I wouldn't mind giving him an extra recommendation since I knew both him and his potential employer, which I gladly did.

Now Dean couldn't have known or foreseen this scenario. He just treated me like I was in his Front Row for the weekend. He didn't need to make any extra effort to befriend me on that visit. In fact, thousands of students there didn't make that extra effort, but he did.

There wasn't any ulterior motive; he didn't get paid anything because I chose to attend school there. He just genuinely cared and wanted me to have a great experience. He put me in his Front Row for that weekend. Because of that, I did everything I could to help him out when he needed it and I was in a position to do so.

# CHAPTER 14

# The Bribe That Made Me a 4.0 Student

T his story happened in high school, but the lesson translated into college. As I mentioned earlier, my parents wanted to keep me on the straight and narrow. They bribed me. I really wanted my own car, so they said, "If you play some sport every year of high school, we'll help you pay for your first car."

Of course I chose cross-country because it was the lowest contact sport, and I didn't need to try out. What I didn't know was that at my school all the cross-country kids were smart. Like really smart. AP students galore. I didn't care to be friends with any of them because I had all my skate friends. But soon enough, I started doing really well in cross-country and I kind of had to spend time with these guys.

I never considered myself overly intelligent, but something changed. By my junior year, I became an AP class kid too. I hung around all these guys who had such high expectations of themselves that I simply wanted to be better. They respected me because I was fast, and I respected them because they were smart, and soon enough their smartness wore off on me.

In my senior year our cross-country team was ranked number two in the entire state of California with the highest average GPA per varsity runner. We received the Scholastic Athlete Achievement Award in front of the entire school. Sure some people probably thought we were kind of lame, but I didn't care. My life changed because my friends changed.

That fall semester, my senior year of high school was the first time I earned a 4.0 report card, which actually helped me get an additional scholarship to the college of my choice. In the end, my parents didn't have the money to help me pay for that car, but what I got out of changing my relationship environment taught me a valuable lesson:

---

*If you want to get good grades, hang out with people who get good grades. If you don't care about your grades, hang out with people who don't care about their grades.*

---

Obviously college isn't only about your GPA, but the lesson is sound. What do you want? Who's doing that already? How can you hang around them? I'll restate it.

*Does being around this person make me want to be a better person?*

There are no perfect people on this planet, especially in college. However, you have a choice who you let into your life and who you allow to influence you. And if it were in your control, who would you rather spend time with?

## TIPS TO CHANGE YOUR RELATIONSHIP ENVIRONMENT

1. **Join something.** Like in the above example, by default, joining a sport or a club with a certain group of people will change your social opportunities. Use the rule of proximity in your favor. It can be a little awkward joining a new group, but remember everything is new until it isn't. Relationships take time to grow and the more time you spend around certain groups of people, the more you'll find it easier to connect with them.

2. **Study Groups.** This was a lifesaver for me in college. I'll discuss this in detail in the section about grades, but my study buddies became some of my best friends, and we

stayed very close as the years went on and we entered more specific upper-division classes.

3. **Talk to strangers.** When you were a little kid, people probably told you the opposite. Now that you're a grown up, learning to talk with strangers can open up your horizons. It takes guts to walk up to someone you don't know. Just find an excuse. Find a question to ask. Lean into discomfort, and you'll be amazed what you find on the other side.

# CHAPTER 15

# The One Skill That Will Turn Dreams into Reality

---

Imagine this:

How would it feel to know that when you graduate you could have any job you wanted?

How would it feel to know that you could attract and keep the most desirable significant other?

How would it feel if, whenever you expressed an idea, people listened intently?

How would it feel if you could convince your parents to let you do something they've never let you do before?

I think you'd agree, all of these things would be amazing. Too good to be true?"

Not if you learn this one skill.

What skill?

The skill of *selling yourself*.

## WHAT SELLING IS NOT

I remember a friend introducing me to her boyfriend. We'll call him Jake.

Jake was a sharp guy attending an excellent school. He was a business major.

I asked him if he'd had any sales experience, to which he snobbily replied, "Sales! I'm not a salesman. I'm a business major."

Sadly, Jake's attitude is shared by a lot of students, whether they're business majors or not. And those students are setting themselves up for a very tough road after college.

Most people think selling is "convincing someone to do something they don't want to do." Far from it.

*Sales is merely your ability to influence people to make a decision or take action.*

Have you ever watched a great movie then told a friend about it? If your excitement convinced them to see the movie, then that's a sale. You influenced them to make a decision and to take action. Didn't it feel awesome?

We love to influence. Our friend is now happier because we sold them on seeing the movie, and they loved it.

Another way to look at it is this: *Sales is expressing what you believe in such a way that others want to believe it. too.*

If you're passionate about a topic or a cause, your ability to convince other people to see the world the way you see it is selling. Your ability to express your beliefs so that others can understand them will truly allow you to be a powerful force for change.

## WHY IS THIS RELEVANT TO YOU?

If you want to do something significant with your life, you'll need the support of other people. If you want those people to buy into your ideas and beliefs, they first must buy into you. You need to sell them on you!

## THE ART OF SELLING YOURSELF

Whenever we meet someone for the first time, we ask ourselves two questions:

1.  Do I like this person?
2.  Can I trust them?

Think about it. When you meet someone for the first time, notice where you go mentally. Don't you look for consistencies? We want to know if this person is honest. We want to know if what they are saying is true. How do we feel when we're around them?

# LIKABILITY

It's a fact that when we like someone we are more apt to listen to whatever they have to say. When we like someone we are more likely to do a favor for them. We want to introduce people we like to others because we assume our friends will like them, too.

Likability is an extraordinary trait that can take you far in life and is critical if we want to sell ourselves. When others like us, it becomes much easier to influence them one way or another.

Think about who you like and who you follow on Instagram or Twitter. We allow those we like to speak to us. We give them our time and attention. If we didn't like them, we'd simply ignore them. We want to follow those who we like and respect.

To learn to increase your likability, read the book, *The Likeability Factor*, by Tim Sanders or listen to the podcast *The Art of Likability* by Arel Moodie.

# TRUST

Trust will always outweigh likability when it comes to influencing.

Think about the president of the United States. Not necessarily the specific person in the oval office right now, but the position of the president.

If the president of the United States walked into your house and said, "There are space aliens attacking Earth, and you need to come with me if you want to live." You'd probably go with them. Why would they lie?

Now take one of your friends whom you "don't trust" as much. You know, the one who always says one thing, then does another. The one who constantly talks big but acts small. Maybe you notice her talk about people behind their backs and then be nice to their face.

Let's replay that alien scenario with that person instead of the president. Wouldn't you hesitate? You'd start off with, "Is this a joke, like when you said..."

It's an uphill battle when we don't trust someone or when others don't trust us.

How do you develop trust?

Simple: Follow through consistently on what you say you will do and take responsibility when you can't.

Think about a car. What is the car's job? To drive. What happens when the car breaks down? Its reliability or "ability to be counted on" is compromised. If it keeps breaking down, what's your experience of that car? Would you recommend that same make or model of car to friends or family? Probably not. Now, you might continue driving that car if you need to, but only until you can afford to buy a new one. A reliable one.

Consider that you and I are the same as that car.

Relationships are a series of agreements and promises. Some are spoken, some are assumed. If you tell someone you'll be there at a certain time, but repeatedly show up late with excuses, their ability to trust your word diminishes. When we start breaking promises with people, we start to become that unreliable car. People lose trust in us.

Why is this important to you?

When we move into the real world, the world where stakes are higher, a world where we want people to pay us good money for doing a job, if people do not like us or trust us, we will be stuck taking what's given rather than getting what we want.

You might be thinking, *I'm just a student. I've got time. This isn't important now. I'll do it later.* I thought the same thing, and so do most students. However, you're not reading this book because you want to be like *most students.* You want an advantage that's going to position you to get your dream job out of college.

There's one more way to grow your trust and influence, and I devoted the entire next section to the topic because I think it's so important.

If you do this next thing correctly, you'll be able to start your journey into that dream life before you ever get your degree.

# CHAPTER 16

# Borrowed Influence

L et's say you're trying to make brownies, and the recipe calls for sugar, but you don't have any. You know your neighbor, that sweet old lady, is always baking something. What do you do? You could go to the store like most people and buy it, or you could go next door and ask her for a cup. If you did the latter, what you'd find is she'd probably be happy to share what she has a surplus of. Why am I telling you this?

When you're breaking into the job market, you won't have much influence, but other people will. *The way you learn to have influence and credibility with many, is to have influence and credibility with some.*

This is called borrowed influence.

The funny thing with so many ambitious people is they feel they have to do everything themselves. What I learned early in my skateboarding and college careers is that leveraging borrowed influence is the fastest way to get what we want.

I'm going to let you in on a secret. As a semiprofessional skateboarder, I was good but not that good. There were plenty of other kids out there much better than me. But I learned how to borrow the influence of my friends who were much better than I was.

Once I went to a contest where a bunch of industry people were in attendance. A few of my friends were sponsored by one particular company, and I was interested in them, too. The team manager's name was Dave.

I asked a friend to introduce me to Dave, we chatted for a little bit, and then I told him how I'd love to ride for his company one day. These guys get hit up all the time by kids wanting free product. Usually you have to send them a video to prove that you are as good as you say you are. When I asked Dave if he'd like me to send him my video he said with a smile, "No, that's okay, man. I imagine if you're friends with these guys, you're good in my book."

*Seriously? That's it?* I thought.

Purely because of whom I was associated with, I bypassed everyone else in line.

That is the power of borrowed influence. Because you hang around people who are respected and admired, you will become respected and admired.

Eventually you will have to perform. If you can't perform to a certain level, you will make yourself and the person who introduced you look bad. Fortunately, when Dave actually saw me skate, I was good enough to stay on the team.

When you associate yourself with the right people, and if they have good things to say about you, new opportunities will open up. If you want to learn how to apply this principle to any industry or job search, you'll love the next two sections.

# CHAPTER 17

# Who Needs an Interview?

F ox Business news states that 69 percent of high paying jobs are acquired through a personal referral. Now, some people have those connections immediately, but I never did.

It's not just about who you know, it's about who knows you and *what they know about you.*

What is an interview? It's an assessment of whether you are worthy for the job at hand. Well, what if you considered this: *Your interview starts TODAY, and every person in your life is a potential employer.*

Now this doesn't mean that you have to be fake and phony, never showing weakness, and never making a mistake. All this statement should do is raise your awareness that every person you meet may be a connection for the future job or career.

It's a mistake that most students make growing up. Not realizing that the people in their lives—adults, peers, even underclassmen—will be in a different place 10 years from now, and they may be in a position to help you.

Famed business philosopher Jim Rohn once stated, "People may not remember what you did or said, but they remember how you made them feel."

That statement goes a long way when you prepare to make a full transition into the marketplace. What impression do you leave with most people?

A mentor once told me, "Be a hard master on yourself now, and life will be easy, or be an easy master on yourself (that is, do what feels good in the moment), and life will be hard."

HERE IS THE GOLDEN NUGGET: *Do anything that will positively distinguish YOU from everyone your age.*

People notice.

When you come in for a job, employers don't like to go through the hours, days, weeks, and months of interviews to find the right person. Why? If you start acting as if there is no one like you, you won't blend in with everyone else, and the process of finding a job through the traditional interview process will either be shortened or eliminated altogether.

CHAPTER 18

# Getting a Mentor— Breaking into Any Industry

All this relationship building leads up to one of the most important access points to gain entry into your real-world dream job. Here is a strategy I have personally used and taught to students all across the country to help them break into ANY industry. It takes a little research, preparation, practice, and guts. But it works!

## STEP 1: RESEARCH

Take the time to look at the companies and people in the industries that you are curious about. Don't just think about the biggest, baddest companies in the industry. Look around at some of the smaller operations. Those people have fewer barriers to entry and are often more open-minded to sitting down with students.

Learn as much as you can about each company and look through their board of directors or employees. Make a list of the one to three people you might like to meet.

## STEP 2: CONTACT

Email is the easiest. If the contact information is not available on the website, try calling the company and asking like this:

*"Hi I was wondering if you could help me. I'm a student at _____, and I'm considering a career in _____. Who's the person that runs everything over there?*

*I was really hoping to interview them about getting into that field and what it's like. Could I get their email address from you?"*

Send a letter or an email for potential interview:

*"Hi _____, I hear you are the man or woman I need to talk to. I am a student at _____ and am really curious about getting into _____. It would be an honor to treat you to coffee or lunch some time just to ask you questions about the field and how you got to where you are.*

*Would you be willing to spare some time? I'd really appreciate it."*

Not everyone will be interested or willing to meet with you. That's ok. We don't need everyone to say yes, just a few. When you get a yes or two, do these next few things to make sure your meeting is worthwhile and memorable.

Super Ninja move— Call back the front desk person:

*"Hi _____, this is _____. I don't know if you remember, but I'm the student from _____. We spoke (time) ago about interviewing _____."*

*Well, they decided to meet with me. Thanks so much for your help.*

*I wondered if you could answer a few questions for me about _____, so I'm better prepared for our meeting? Do you have a minute?*

*Where did _____ go to college?*

*What did he/she study?*

*Is there anything I should bring up or ask about, or NOT ask about?*

*Outside of work what are _____ hobbies or interests?"*

When we talk about positioning and situating yourself as someone who is different than anyone else your age, this is what it looks like. Who does this kind of stuff? No one! Except for you. Because you're awesome.

If you are worried that you are being too nosy, what you'll actually find is that even the front desk person will start to think, "Dang... I hope this kid gets a job here someday. We need more people like him."

## STEP 3: MEET

It's best to meet in a public place, like a coffee shop or restaurant. I like coffee shops because there is no awkward eating time when you'd like to be talking. But if they offer to go to lunch, of course take them up on it.

Side note: I always offer to pay out of respect. Not always, but often they won't let you and will pay because they are impressed with your initiative. Never assume this, though. I once sat with a person I highly respected who charges hundreds and sometimes thousands of dollars for his time. When I offered to pay he said "Thanks." The experience was well worth the $30.

Bring a pen and paper. It's more professional than taking notes on your phone.

Here are some questions to ask on the interview:

1. Why did you choose to go into _____?
2. I heard you went to _____? Why did you go to that school?
3. What was your degree in?
4. Did you ever change your major?
5. What were your hardest classes?
6. What was surprisingly harder than you thought when getting into the field?
7. What's your favorite part of what you do?

8. What sacrifices have you had to make to get where you are?

9. If you could do it all over, what would you do differently?

10. Do you ever offer internships at your firm/office/company?

11. Would you be willing to allow me to come visit the office/factory some time?

12. What's a question no one ever asks you about _____ that you wish they would? (I have to give credit to my friend Jon Vroman for this nugget of a question.)

Now you don't need to ask all these questions, especially not in this order. But take the time to write down the questions you want answers to.

## STEP 4: SCHEDULE FOLLOW-UP ACTIONS

Make notes of actions that you need to take. Ask if it's all right to follow up with them as you progress in semesters and years.

Don't expect immediate job offers because you did this. You proved that you're hungry by arranging this whole shindig, and now you need to prove you're worth a future meeting.

## STEP 5: STAY IN TOUCH

Find excuses and reasons to reach out. Maybe you find an interesting article you think they might appreciate, or maybe you see them in the news or in an online publication. Shoot them an email with a screen shot or copy of what you found. It doesn't need to be a long email. Something as simple as, "I saw this and it reminded me of our conversation. Hope you are well." It's a little thing, but remember this... most people don't do the little things. It's the little things that will give you the edge over everyone your age. Take the time. It's worth it.

You don't have to have a formal structure set up with mentors, including weekly scheduled or structured meetings or calls. Some relationships will blossom into that, and that's great. Most of my mentors were like this: A one-time meeting. Follow-up emails. Maybe I'd send them a book or gift around the holidays. Then another meeting if I'm looking to take action in the industry or if I need a referral.

## STEP 6: MAKE THE REQUEST

Now if you did the above things correctly, you will find that opportunities start to open up. Again, the goal is to do anything you can to distinguish yourself from everyone you'll be competing against. Few people take the initiative to meet with a potential employer years before they need the job.

When the time comes, reach out to your contacts and tell them you are ready.

Here's a sample email:

*I wanted to let you know that I'll be graduating this coming spring and I'm ready to make some moves into the industry. I'm very excited and grateful for all the time and advice you've given me. Especially about (fit in something specific here). It has made all the difference.*

*I was wondering if you'd be willing to connect me with anyone in (the industry) that might have opportunities opening up.*

That's it. Pretty simple. In fact, they were probably expecting or hoping you'd reach out. If you really wowed them, they probably have already spoken with friends and associates about you. They may offer you something at their own company or walk you through the front door to a great connection.

I talked to a parent who did these exact steps with their daughter when she was interested in aeronautics as a high schooler. She looked up someone who worked for NASA, scheduled time to meet, asked all the good questions, and stayed in touch throughout college. BOOM! Guess who landed a job at NASA when she graduated.

You don't have to be in high school or even a college freshman to do these things. You could be 50 years old and all of these strategies would work. The point is that you are Pro-active. Set yourself up for success by taking these actions now, wherever you are, instead of waiting until you need a job and have to sit down with all the other applicants applying for the same position.

Make the investment in these relationships, and you will see your ideal future come to fruition.

# PART FOUR
# Academics

# CHAPTER 19

# Don't Trade Grades for Learning

## LEARNING TO LEARN

### Liam Kyle Cahill, University of Nevada Reno

"Get good grades." That's the standard. That's the bar. The funny thing is, I've never found that to be very difficult (or useful) at all.

I'm an average guy with an average brain, but I happen to have the ability to make people think I'm smarter than I am. I've skated through every level of schooling from kindergarten to college, and I owe it all to the teachers and parents who told me that I needed to get good grades at an early age. Next I investigated what it took to make these people happy with the least amount of effort possible... after all I had sports, friends, TV, and of course video games to demand my time. Let me be clear that the objective I had wasn't to learn, but instead to get straight A's.

My strategy was simple and works at every grade level: Don't miss class, ask lots of questions, get the teacher to know my name (asking questions certainly helps), and make friends with the smartest kids in class. The last part is key. Getting the right people to want to help you is truly the best thing you can do to succeed in anything!

It's not that I don't care about learning, it's that I just never needed to. My recipe worked so well that I finished high school with a GPA above 4.0 (adjusted for AP courses) and received my bachelor's degree in Hydrogeology above a 3.5 GPA. I finished the pinnacle of what many people say matters: getting good grades and having a college degree. But now what? I had to get a job.

I found the real world to be very different from the school world I was accustomed to. There were no longer cheat sheets with relevant formulas or answer keys to make you feel all warm and fuzzy when you got something 90% correct. The idealized situations found on tests and in our textbooks were nothing more than fantasy compared to the complexity of variables usually found in real life. For the first time I found myself struggling *because I had never learned how to learn* while in school. I was too focused on getting good grades.

After four years working jobs relevant to my degree, I've taken a new path and have finally found my passion: Music. Every day I get to pick up my instrument and learn something new. The best part is that now I get paid for it. Let that sink in. I get paid to learn and do what I love. Now don't get me wrong, I work harder than I ever have before, but it's easier to do when you're passionate about it.

---

The reason I started off with Liam's story is because he is right on the money with what so many students mistake as the sole purpose of college. Grades. Not that grades aren't important but they aren't everything. They are designed to be a reflection of what you have learned and what you know.

However, when all we learn is how to impress people rather than internalizing the information so that it's useful later on, we miss the point.

This is why the last section we went through on connections and relationships is so important because when you take the time to meet and speak with someone who is doing what you want to do, you learn to find the classes and knowledge that will be necessary to succeed in your field. Not just because it's a part of the curriculum for graduating with your degree, but because you see how it directs your thinking and sets you up for the career you want.

I went to a liberal arts university and was required to take seemingly random classes like seventeenth century French History. Like when am I going to need to know the year that Napoleon Bonaparte lost the battle of Waterloo? Maybe when I'm on Jeopardy. *The answer is "what is 1815?" Mr. Trebek.* Still waiting for my invitation to be on the show. Anyways...

The purpose of some classes is not just to teach you mindless information, although it will often seem like that. These classes are designed to round you out. I loved that Liam said he "hadn't learned how to learn" and I would assert that many students are in that same place.

So how do you make the most of the academic side of the college experience?

My answer to maximizing the learning opportunity in college is simple:

1. Become curious
2. Find your learning style

## CURIOSITY

Curiosity is the precursor to learning. If someone is not curious about what they are studying, that class will be a complete bore. Sometimes the teachers teaching style can influence that, but when you become curious and hungry to learn, it's amazing what you start to pick up.

Here's my challenge to you: Can you find something fascinating with every class, every topic, and every teacher?

Ask yourself, what's interesting about this topic? What's unusual? Where will I apply this later in my life?

If you have trouble finding an answer, here's a strategy that few students will take and it's one that will absolutely transform your experience of being in the classroom.

Ask these questions of your professors. Why is this important? What do they find interesting, unusual, fascinating about this topic? How do they apply it in their lives? You'd be amazed at the answers.

# ACCIDENTAL FAVORITE CLASS

Mass Communications 101 was a class I accidentally took my senior year. I thought it would help me with my communication and public speaking skills, but it turned out to be a class about how companies and corporations use different types of mediums like TV, radio, and the internet to communicate with the masses.

At first I thought, "Man, this isn't at all what I thought it was going to be about." However, I was locked in for four months with this teacher and since it was my senior year, I thought, "Well, I better make the most of it."

I wound up having coffee with my professor and asked him the above questions. His answers blew my mind.

He went on to tell me about all the products and companies that he's worked with and sold. He shared with me stories of flying to Japan and learning the etiquette to communicate with different cultures in a business setting. I learned that he had his own radio show and even had his own company that sold the music you listen to when you are on hold with a customer service line. He was the voice that said, "Thank you for waiting. An agent will be with you shortly. By the way, did you know that..." then he'd go on to mentioning other products the company offered. It made those companies a lot of money, and consequently made him a lot of money. He taught my class for the fun of it. This was an interesting guy and my respect grew for him and what I was learning.

Bottom line, he showed me a much bigger world that his class applied to. Mass Communication became one of my favorite classes in my entire college experience.

Most students don't take the initiative or responsibility to become curios about their classes. It's *just one of those things* you have to go through to get that diploma. I was like that for most of college, but as soon as I learned how to ask good questions and be responsible for my learning experience, it was a whole different ball game.

# FIND YOUR LEARNING STYLE

Everyone learns differently. This is commonly an issue with students who have never taken the time to learn how they learn best.

There are several studies that show the different ways that people learn so let's lay out the most common:

**VISUAL**— Watch and learn

**AUDITORY**— Listen and learn

**KINESTHETIC**— Do and learn

**READING/WRITING**— Read and learn

And when it comes to studying, are you best by yourself or studying in a group?

We can learn through each of these styles, but everyone has preferences for how they pick up and practice information.

I'm visual and auditory. If someone tells me and shows me, I am much more likely to understand a topic. Classroom settings with PowerPoints, videos, and lecture are very easy for me to learn in. However, when it came to studying, I had a really hard time picking up a book and reading by myself. I also learn best in a group setting. It took me a while to figure this out, but eventually I spent most of my time with people who read the book and had them tell me what they learned. Some might think this is cheating or being lazy, but it's just how I learned best.

There are people who could care less about being in the classroom, and they're better off sitting by themselves in the library and just reading the book.

Some people need to apply the knowledge by using it or acting it out such as in a lab or working on a physical project.

There's no right or wrong way to learn, and this is important because you will have friends who get great grades and they learn/study completely different from you. Don't judge yourself for this or wish you were different. Instead, start aligning yourself with how you learn best.

There are several on-line assessments to help you figure out how you learn best. Here are a few:

*www.EducationPlanner.org*

*www.HowToLearn.com*

*www.Learning-styles-online.com*

The best thing for you to do is pay attention for how you learn best. When do you enjoy learning most? When do you feel the most comfortable absorbing information? Learning is a personal thing and it's important to find what works best for you.

# CHAPTER 20

# Putting the "F" in Freshman

L et me share with you one of my first struggles academically during my Freshman year.

The "F" in freshman could stand for the new-found freedom of the college experience. The "F" in freshman could also stand for the grade you'll get if that freedom is not respected.

I was no exception.

In high school I worked pretty hard to get into college, and once I made it I thought I'd be able to just cruise on through. Not so much!

Because I was taking a full load of science classes, my first semester was a bigger challenge than I had expected. At the mid-point of the semester, I was failing one of my science classes so badly that if I aced everything the rest of the semester, a "C" was the best I could hope for. The teacher had a voice that was easy to fall asleep to. I mean he could have made a lot of money selling recorded versions of his lectures to insomnia patients. But I'm not bitter. He just didn't hit my auditory learning style, plus there was a ton of reading which wasn't my strong point. Eventually I chose to withdraw.

That "W" on my transcript didn't affect my GPA, but it did give a shock to my system, causing me to take every semester after that very seriously.

I hadn't yet figured out my learning style. After reflecting on my classes that did go well I discovered that I learn best in a group setting where we can discuss ideas and or look at videos/diagrams that explain the information.

Of course, I still read the books as best I could, but as soon as I stopped judging myself for not being the best reader, I became such a better student and even started enjoying those classes previously deemed impossible.

You'll have professors who's teaching styles don't jive with your learning styles. The point is not to blame them but to take responsibility for your own education. It's to accept your learning style and find a way to apply that to every class. It will probably require you to talk to your professor and ask him for help. Share with him or her how you learn best and ask for any recommendations.

Remember *the professor works for you. You pay the tuition bill.* Most professors care and want to see you succeed and will take the time with you. There are always a few oddballs who try to push people out of the class, but it's less than most students think.

Complaining will get you nowhere academically.

Take responsibility, own your learning, and you'll be amazed at how your academic experience changes.

Getting used to the level of academic work in college is mind boggling. While grades are not the most important thing in college, they do matter. Let's dive deeper into finding your motivation to succeed in the classroom.

# CHAPTER 21

# Finding Your Motivation— The $10 per hour Principle

<br>

**W**hat if every semester of college that you received straight "A's," it would add $10 per hour to your future income?

Meaning, if you ace your first two semesters of college, at a minimum you'd be guaranteed $20 an hour in income. That might not sound too exciting, but let's take it further. What if you graduated in four years. That's an extra $20/hour you'd add each year if you kept those grades up. If you make $80/hour at a 40 hour work week over 50 weeks in a year, that means you are earning: $160,000/year. Not bad. If you look at grad school, or add a Ph.D., those numbers could go even higher.

Unfortunately we can't quantify income this way. There is no one who will pay you an extra $10 per hour for every straight-A report card, but it does raise an interesting question: If this were true, would you do everything in your power to get straight A's?

Of course you would. We all would.

Whatever your distinguishing factor is, you could be a straight-A student if you wanted to.

Remember something: We are not paid for our time, but for the value we bring in that time.

The value of getting good grades will influence your value to the marketplace in two ways:

1. It shows you are willing to work hard to be the best, to get the grades.

2. It shows you are highly competent and above average (again, whatever separates you from the pack). A student who gets higher grades is likely (not always) going to be more knowledgeable about a topic and thus, more valuable.

Now I was not a straight "A" student in college, and I'm not saying that you need to be in order to be successful. However, if we make it a goal and an objective and we miss the mark, we'll be better off than if we didn't care like so many other students.

Here are a few strategies from students I met who truly excelled academically in college.

---

# ONE "B"

### Amiee Mueller

My dad would tell anyone who'd listen how his daughter earned one "B" in college, and follow that up with, "The rest were all A's!" Though grades are not the only gauge of academic success, they are one indicator. Plus, they led to positive outcomes I hadn't expected, such as being offered a research position by one of my professors, a teaching aid position by another, and an academic scholarship my final year of college.

I'm not a genius, and I didn't go to a highly rated school K-12. What I am is committed, observant, and a calendar-owner.

At the beginning of each semester, I'd take all of the syllabi from my professors and consolidate the information into one calendar. Google Calendar is great for this for those who don't want to carry a paper version. Once I had exam dates and project due dates noted, I'd go back through and write in when I needed to start working on each project. As the semester progressed, I'd add things that came up such as study sessions or group meetings. Then all I had to do was follow it, aka, actually implement it.

It also helped to pay attention to who the other top students in the class were and foster study groups with them. Since each person possesses different strengths, it makes sense that everyone does better when they work together. Going through class material or reviewing subjects as a group can have a positive impact on overall understanding of the material.

In my Literary Analysis class, for which we did a good amount of reading and writing, our professor gave us an assignment. We were to find a partner who would read our papers and provide feedback, which we'd then use to improve our work before turning in the assignments.

On the day we'd choose our partners, I sat next to the student whose papers were often cited aloud by the teacher as an example of great work. When it came time to pair up, it was a simple "Want to work together?" that begin our partnership. For the rest of that semester, we each helped the other take our writing to a higher level. It was a fabulous partnership that I still look back on with fondness. And it all began with simply paying attention to who was performing well in class.

Lastly, it helps to attend classes. Missing classes is easy, fun, and may be unavoidable on rare occasion, but doing it too often can lead to unnecessary academic challenges.

------

# THE TWENTY-FIRST CENTURY STRUGGLE

*Learn to say NO to your distractions NOW,*
*or prepare to say NO to your family later when they*
*ask you to put food on the table because you lacked the*
*discipline to create a better life for yourself.*
*Get to work while you're young.*
*—Joseph Diaz*

In the context of achieving a goal, we must decide and *go*. I once heard someone say, success is merely remembering what you want and why you want it.

The biggest challenge that college students today face, and what will be the subtle killer of your future possibilities if you don't master it, is this: FOCUS.

Earlier I shared with you the story of one of my favorite classes in college called Mass Media Communications. That professor spent years in advertising and marketing and he taught us a principle that I remember to this day. You are not the customer of mass television and internet providers. Businesses and corporations are the customers.

Who do you think pays all the actors of your favorite TV shows? Not you. The companies who buy the advertising do. They have such an ornate understanding of the psychology of capturing and keeping attention that you don't even notice it. Have you ever been watching something from a DVR when you could easily skip through the commercials, but you don't realize it until you are two or three commercials in? That's a good commercial. It captured and retained your attention.

The reason they do this is obvious. They want you to buy their stuff.

The greatest battle you face on a daily basis is the one for your attention. If it's worth those companies paying millions of dollars to media groups, it sure better be important to you.

The one thing you will never run short of in college is distractions. I'm not saying you need to throw away your Xbox or never watch TV, but realize that you need to master your distractions or they will master you.

# CHAPTER 22

# E vs E— The Ratio That Will Transform Your Productivity

I credit author and speaker Brian Tracy with sharing the E vs E ratio with me.

What is the E vs E ratio?

Entertainment vs Education

If you added it all up, what percentage of your time are you entertaining yourself versus educating yourself? Our cell phones, tablets, and computers are nonstop distraction devices. Emails, Facebook, Twitter, Instagram, Vine, SnapChat, and so on all vie for our attention.

Of course, there is some educational value here, but if we're being honest with ourselves, they are huge distractions.

Your success in life will be in direct proportion to your ability to focus your attention on preparing and educating yourself to achieve your goals. Here's a simple challenge. Do this for a week.

In your phone, make a note every 15 minutes of what you did. From eating, being on your phone, reading a textbook, going to the bathroom, talking on the phone, texting, spacing out, etc.

The numbers will astound you. There will likely be a big difference between how much time you think you spend doing something and how much time you actually spend. Just the simple awareness of how you spend your time should make a dramatic shift in your activity.

# 6. FIVE TIPS FOR STAYING DISTRACTION-FREE IN COLLEGE

1. **Turn off Wi-Fi on phone or computer while working.** If you can't access the internet, you won't be tempted.

2. **Delete the apps from your phone while you're studying.** You can always re-download them for free when you are ready.

3. **Make a public declaration that you will not be on Facebook, Twitter...** for whatever length of time and inform people that if something is really important to call you.

4. **Delete people from your phone.** This is a hard one, but I found myself being the instigator of a lot of time wasting by calling people on the phone. I deleted certain people's phone numbers from my phone and wrote them down so if I really needed to call them I could. This saved me a lot of time.

5. **Turn off and hide your phone.** If it's out of sight, and out of sound, it's out of mind

6. **Plan entertainment time.** Make playing video games or social media a reward when you are done. Pay the price first, reward yourself second.

6.5. **Practice saying "Yes, when..."** It's easy to make this decision to study a priority yourself, but then there's everyone else in your life. Become better at saying "Yes, when I'm done with _____". They will respect you and if they don't, they don't deserve to be in your front row or your phone.

## ACADEMIC PLANNING

I remember hearing, "An hour of preparation will save you two hours in execution." I don't know if that's factually true, but it does illustrate a point. Take the time to prepare, and it will save you time in living the busy life as a student. Instead of reacting at the last minute to life, like most students do, you'll be composed, patient, and most importantly, relaxed. Luck favors the prepared mind.

Taking the time to plan out all your classes, projects, papers, tests, events, etc., will make college life *much* easier.

When I was a senior and my skateboarding trips and work life started taking off, I had to know my schedule months in advance. I saw conflicts with the testing schedule in some of my classes and was able to approach my professors early in the year versus the week of the exam.

I remember walking up to my psychology teacher two weeks into the semester to discuss a scheduling conflict I was going to have two months into the semester. The professor was floored. How many students do you think she had that were organized and professional enough to bring this up to her so early in the year? Of course, she granted me permission to miss that day of class and allowed me to take the test early.

I wasn't always like this. In fact, I'd say I was pretty disorganized most of my life. However, now I was playing a bigger game with my life. I was pursuing my passion of professional skateboarding and taking on a full load as a student and I was working. You can't do all those things flying by the seat of your pants.

We all have the same amount of time in the day; it's up to us to choose how we use it.

Here's a lesson from Harvard graduate Michael Coscetta about how he planned each academic semester for both personal and professional growth.

## GETTING IT ALL DONE
### Michael Coscetta, Harvard

To most people, college means classes, regimen, writing, and reading—generally things that don't always translate to fun, especially for a teenager. So to me college had to be more than just school. I always believed that you could get an education anywhere and at any time, but you only have one time to go to college. College was going to be a life experience, and an experience that years and decades later I'd be able to reflect on with nostalgia as well as with satisfaction. I needed to make sure that I saw the big picture and that I lived life in college and didn't let college become my life. Of course, it was imperative to me that I get good grades and to take care of my requirements, but I wanted to do more.

I wanted to meet new people, many new people. I wanted to try new things, to explore new places, to do the things that most college students claim they never had time to do. I was fortunate enough to attend a school that magnified the impact of these experiences. However, I needed to be very intentional about my schedule and my decisions to be able to incorporate all of these goals into my life, while also getting very good grades. Every month I created a new list of goals, some physical (working out, etc.), some relational (join a new club/activity, organize a dinner), and some experiential (attend a seminar, go to a speech at the Institute of Politics). These goal lists reminded me of what I had set out to accomplish, and they forced me to constantly think about my experience.

In the process of living this superior college life, I found out that I had several passions outside of academics. These passions have driven my non-vocational goals ever since, and I think my post-college life has been that much more fulfilling because of the decisions I made while in school. A key lesson from my four years in college was to take advantage of every opportunity presented to me. If I was introduced to a new person, I immediately set out to make a new friend. If a guest speaker was coming to visit Harvard, I signed up right away. If we had a week off, I tried to organize a trip somewhere. Everyone has opportunities in life, and I wanted to make sure I took advantage of the ones in front of me. Of course, looking back, I think I could have done a lot more, seen a lot more, and met a lot more people, but hindsight is 20/20, and that's why I am sharing my experience here. Be intentional about taking advantage of every opportunity you have in college, and make sure that your time in college is about more than just books and learning.

---

*Your success after college will be in direct proportion to how much opportunity you took advantage of while in college.*

---

## *YOU* ARE YOUR FIRST PRIORITY

Are you overwhelmed yet? Stress is no stranger to college students. It's important to remember that you are human, not a machine—although you might feel like it at times.

There is enough time to do *anything* you want, not *everything* you want. There is no perfect solution to this whole college thing. Some semesters will be harder than others based on the level of classes and intensity of study required.

It will feel at times that you are going to crack. To help you make it through these hard times, make sure that you take time for yourself, your passions, and for your health.

My friend and health expert Joe Utley always told me, "Health is your first wealth." It doesn't make sense to work so hard to make a lot of money only to spend all that money fixing what you did to your body.

Hal Elrod, author of the best-selling book *The Miracle Morning: The Not-So-Obvious Secret Guaranteed to Transform Your Life (Before 8AM)*, shares his daily success rituals to help people achieve peak performance. He came up with this morning routine after going through severe depression in his mid-20s. He'd lost thousands of dollars in a bad business deal and owed more on his house than it was worth.

He realized that he couldn't go on this way much longer, so he took the time to list out what he was doing when he was happiest in his life. There were certain habits that, when he did them consistently, made a tremendous difference. I highly recommend that you buy his book and read it. With his permission, I'd like to share with you his Life S.A.V.E.R.S. formula that transformed my life and does for thousands of high achievers and students who are prone to overwhelm.

# THE LIFE S.A.V.E.R.S. FORMULA

**Silence:** Take the time to sit in silence and quiet the mind for three, five, or ten minutes. Our minds are often like a snow globe. When you shake it up, the snow flies everywhere. That happens all day long for us. When we take the time to sit in silence, all the craziness and concerns we have start to melt away. This quiet is a great place from which to start the day.

**Affirmations:** Do you realize that you talk to yourself? Right now if you're wondering *Do I talk to myself?* you have the answer. We all do. Sadly, most of our internal commentary reminds us of the mistakes we've made and why we shouldn't even try. Taking the time to write all your goals down and reading them to yourself every day can make a profound difference by simply reinforcing and reminding yourself of the end game, what you're working so hard to achieve. Everyone needs a coach to encourage them. Sometimes it has to be ourselves.

**Visualization:** It is a proven fact that visualizing the outcome you want will increase the likelihood that it will happen. After you've read your goals, imagine yourself achieving those goals. How will it feel? What will it look like? What will it smell like? Picturing yourself performing your presentation in front of the class and imagining it going well will make a huge difference in your execution. Just don't forget to actually practice and prepare.

**Exercise:** Doing some yoga, going for a jog, or playing some basketball releases serotonin into the blood stream, which is the feel good chemical. Even when you don't feel like it, do it! You'll be glad you did, and you'll feel a greater level of energy.

**Reading:** Reading something other than an academic book (like the one you're reading now) will open your mind to new ideas and influence creativity. You can access the experience of those who have gone before you and learn from their mistakes. This can help tremendously when you feel bogged down.

**Scribing:** Getting a journal can make a huge difference in stress level. It is shown that taking the time to write out your feelings and thoughts makes it easier to think logically and make good decisions. Also, it's a great way to flesh things out and work on that plan to take over the world.

To learn more, go to *www.MiracleMorning.com* or find the book on *Amazon.com*.

# CHAPTER 23

# Fully Engaged

*It's not a question of IF you can,
but what are you willing to give up so that you CAN.*

---

As you enter and manage your way through college, there will be endless opportunities that open up. Again it's not about how much you can do, but rather how much you can concentrate on.

The thing to remember about pursuing passions and discovering your path is about your level of engagement with what you take on.

Cal Newport wrote a phenomenal book titled *So Good They Can't Ignore You: Why Skills Trump Passion in the Quest for Work You Love,* and in it he challenges the belief that merely following your passions will make you fulfilled and happy.

This is an important concept I want to highlight because, whether you are still have trouble figuring out what you want to do with your life or you definitely know what you want to do, Cal shared some findings in his book that will help you on that journey.

Cal set out to find and interview people who truly love what they do. What he learned was that few people who loved the job they were in actually planned to be there. What affected peoples work-life happiness was whether they performed meaningful work and did it well—so well in fact that there was a high demand for what they did and that gave them control or power over how often and when they worked. A combination of loving the game and getting good at the game allowed them to control when, where, and how they played the game.

However, very few people, if any, get this job right out of college.

The concept "So Good They Can't Ignore You" comes from a quote from famed comedian Steve Martin who used that term to describe the 10 years of mediocre stand up comedy he performed as he mastered his craft and became impossible to ignore.

## CURIOSITY IS THE ANSWER

Cal says that very few people who love their work started out loving their work. They pursued what they were interested in and became curious the more they learned. We talked about this in the beginning of this academic section.

That curiosity is what drove them on a frenzy to understand and experience all they could on the topic.

Those hours, spent practicing or learning, developed what he calls "Career Capital," a commodity we can cash in to take our careers to the next levels. But how do we find the time to do this while we are students?

Being a professional at anything, takes time, dedication, and everyday practice. Here's the story of a real life rock star making her way through college, managing the chaotic schedule of school life, and living her dream of playing in a famous rock band.

-----

## REAL LIFE SCHOOL OF ROCK

### Lena Zawaideh, University of California, Los Angeles

I can truly say I had a rock star college experience. While pursuing an Economics degree at UCLA, I played drums and sang in an alternative rock band called Bad Things. One morning after an econometrics lecture, I drove to Warner Bros. Records and signed my first record deal. A few months later, I was in New York City, performing on the Jimmy Fallon Show, VH1, and Sirius XM radio. Yesterday, I was strolling through university lecture halls; today, the halls of 30 Rockefeller Plaza, flanked inside an elevator by tonight's guest stars, Lindsey Lohan and Liam Neeson. Tomorrow, headlining Lollapalooza in Chicago. The next, beelining to class for my final exam.

This juggling act continued for five years. My attempt to balance school and a music career, although considerably stressful, taught me firsthand the values of hard work, time management, and resilience. Most importantly, however, it taught me that necessity truly is the mother of invention; with a little bit of creative thinking, we can come up with dozens of ways to achieve the same goal.

For instance, we had rehearsals every day at unpredictable times, so it made attending class very difficult. I would take early morning classes, knowing that my band mates slept in, but if we had an early and/or travel day and I couldn't attend class, I'd have a friend record the lectures. Eternally stuck in LA traffic, I would listen to the voice memos of lectures on the way to rehearsal. Between writing, rehearsing, photo shoots, video shoots, voice lessons, meetings, and performances, I would read lecture notes I imported into iBooks or Evernote on my iPhone. If I was in a hurry, I would import my lecture recordings into the application VLC, which allowed me to play them back at 1.5x or 2x speed. I blocked off weekends as my focused studying time. By setting up these systems, I could make use of every minute of downtime I had.

I would plan which quarters to attend or not attend depending on our touring schedule; or if I felt very audacious, I would enroll in online courses to take on the road. When possible, I would negotiate with professors to allow me to take exams early, in case I had to be in a different city or country on exam day. If we were staying in another city for a prolonged period of time, I would enroll in classes at the local university, and have the classes transferred to UCLA for credit. Over the summer of 2014, Bad Things went on tour throughout America supporting Phantogram, and throughout

Europe supporting Thirty Seconds to Mars. Knowing that I had a few weeks of downtime upon returning to the US, I enrolled in a UCSD course in my hometown of San Diego.

Being flexible and finding pockets of focused productive time—whether minutes or months—were the critical factors in helping me achieve academic success while pursuing my music career.

Though I often considered putting school on hold, the option of *being able to obtain my college education and degree while touring the world was exhilarating.*

I have become better able to manage my time and myself, my fears and limiting beliefs, and my idea of what's possible for people. I'm now graduating summa cum laude, and I'm proud to say that I managed to continue the juggling act without dropping every ball.

---

## SEEK UNCOMMON EXPERIENCES

Uncommon experiences will pay off for you if you're willing to embrace them. What do I mean by this? I mean experiences that not every college student will take on. Most people go through the first part of their lives in much the same way. They do what's safe, what's predictable: go to school, play some sports, and take part in some extracurricular activities. No one wants to be average, but the water is warm so everyone jumps in.

What's great about college is that it's the acceptable time to do things you might not ever do, or ever be able to do, again. The world is so big, our country is so big, and your city is so big that there are opportunities for you on every corner.

Early in this book I challenged you to be willing to sacrifice a bit of your identity or who you think or believe you are—not the good stuff, but the self-limiting stuff. Those things where you say, "Oh, I'd never do something like that." Those are the things you should let go of.

WHY? Because it's outside your comfort zone, and your life begins at the end of your comfort zone.

The end of your comfort zone is where you develop those survival skills. Those "I'll do anything to find a way" skills. It's also where you learn to see the world from another's point of view.

These last few chapters are all about how seeking those uncommon experiences can round out a very fulfilling college experience.

# CHAPTER 24

# Leave

---

O ne of the great things about college is the fresh start with a new campus, new friends, new opportunities. Even after being in that environment for a few years, it's time to leave.

No, I don't mean drop out or transfer. I mean leave, explore the world, study abroad, travel abroad, volunteer abroad. Learn how other parts of the world work.

My one major regret during college was missing the opportunity to study abroad. During junior year, several of my friends went to Florence, Italy, for either the summer, or two full semesters. Hearing all the stories of language barriers, social interactions with locals, odd predicaments, and amazing sights had me feel like I missed out a bit.

I didn't have the money at that time and that study abroad program didn't work with my Exercise Science major scheduled curriculum. But that doesn't mean I didn't want to do it.

One day my best friend calls and tells me his family is planning a trip to Thailand.

I jokingly say, "Can I go?" He says, "Sure, if you can pay for yourself."

I become more curious, "How much?" I ask. After discussing it with his mom, they said about $3,000: $1,000 for a flight, $2,000 for food, lodging, and fun.

Being a more experienced student at the time, I sat down and made a plan. They'd leave by December 22, so I planned when I'd need to have the money for my flight, and how much I'd need to work to make the extra. It was possible.

Since my job selling Cutco was commission paid, I figured how much I'd need to sell above what I needed for basic living expenses. At this time I was 100% on my own. (If you don't make commission, find out how many hours you'd need to pick up, or work extra. It's worth it.)

Long story short, I made the money necessary and had one of the most epic two weeks with my best friend and his family in Thailand. I would do all that extra work in a heart beat for that experience.

Everyone's situation is different, and I don't pretend to know where you or your family is financially. If you want it bad enough, you can find a way.

I had many friends who left to go on service trips in different parts of the US and out of the country, mostly paid for by the generosity of others. Every one of them came back talking about how much they loved it.

Find the time. Find the money. Leave. You'll thank me later. In fact, if you have an awesome traveling story, I'd love if you emailed it to me at *John@SkatingThroughCollege.com.*

There's always some level of risk when taking on uncommon experiences. Let's dissect some of the challenges that hold students back from taking these risks.

## RISKS

*If we define risk as the likelihood of an irreversible negative outcome, inaction is the greatest risk of all.*
—Tim Ferriss, The 4-Hour Workweek

---

Risks are an inevitable part of life. But what is a risk really? It's simply a testing of limits. Most risks I'm talking about, you won't die from. You might get a few bumps and bruises, but you'll survive.

That's where the juice of life is. We don't like to play games when there is no chance of losing. Those are boring games.

If you played one-on-one basketball with someone half your age, you wouldn't feel very accomplished in beating them. If they were your own age, that's a different story. If they were older, more athletic, or more experienced than you, then winning would be a great accomplishment. It's the same activity, but when you add a greater likelihood of risk of losing, the greater the level of happiness you'll experience when you win.

Everything worth doing has a scary part. You could fail. But what is failing anyway? It's feedback. It's information that whatever you did, the way you did it, said it, or the time you did it or said it didn't work. Here are a few student stories about taking risks and failing forward.

## CREATE THE RIGHT RELATIONSHIP WITH FAILURE: PHIL'S STORY

Several years ago I met a man named Phil Tirone. He is the best-selling author of a financial book titled 7 Steps to 720 Credit Score (if you don't know what a credit score is, you should go to his website and learn more www.7stepsto720.com). During our interview, Phil shared with me something I will never forget about failure.

He said, "Failure is inevitable. You just need to get used to it. Increase your frequency of failure, and you'll decrease your fear of failing." Phil was a nerdy kid in high school and wasn't comfortable asking girls out. He saw other people in relationships and so badly wanted one for his own. He thought he was just not good with girls. That's the story he told himself over and over, and he kept proving it to himself every time he was too scared to ask them out. The reality is that Phil was afraid of rejection; but in college he decided he'd get over it.

Phil said, "In college, I started asking out any girl I saw, especially ones who were for sure a no. Girls way out of my league. One time I even asked out a married woman just to see what would happen. Fortunately she said no, but you know what, I got over my fear. I had a lot of no's, and I had a lot of dates. Now I'm happily married to a beautiful woman, and I'm glad I went through that experience so I was confident enough to ask out Ms. Right when the opportunity arose. Failure's not so bad, you just need to get used to it."

Now, I am not condoning asking out married people on dates to overcome your fear of the opposite sex. God knows what would happen if they said yes. However, what Phil did was recognize his self-limiting beliefs and start to take action in spite of whom he had previously known himself to be.

------

# MUSICALLY INCLINED

### Jamar Cobb-Dennard, Western Michigan University

I learned the value of taking risks by being resilient when it came to selecting a field of study in college.

When I was seven years old, I began playing the piano. Not long after, I fell in love with the dream of becoming a professional performer —singing and playing on stage.

I practiced endlessly, and learned how to play eight instruments. I left my family and friends at home in Michigan and took a risk to study at the University of North Carolina School of the Arts when I was 16, which also included some time studying music in Switzerland.

One day during practice, I felt so overwhelmed, I slammed the lid of the piano down, buried my head in my arms, and cried.

I thought I had it all planned out and had it made when I received a scholarship to study jazz and music education at Western Michigan University, until the pressure came flooding down on me. I was a freshman taking sophomore and grad-uate level classes, played for a vocal jazz ensemble, had classical and jazz music requirements, and still had to fulfill the normal general education requirements of a college student. It was too much, and the worst part was that I hated it.

It turns out that the latter was the best choice. I enjoyed business, so I switched my major, and ended up with enough credits in both programs to graduate with a dual degree. I still have a passion for music, and I can enjoy it while making a significant contribution to my city through business, community leadership, and politics.

Without taking a risk and being resilient in the midst of change, I would never have been able to enjoy the life I do today.

I had to make a choice— spend the next four years studying something that my heart was no longer in, or take a risk and choose a new major.

---

# CHAPTER 25

# The Leader's Edge

*Leadership is scarce because few people are willing to go through the discomfort required to lead.*
*—Seth Godin*

---

If there's one uncommonly taken yet totally available opportunity in college, it's leadership. Leadership comes in many different shapes and sizes. You don't need to be the president of the student body to be a leader.

Leaders are the ones who influence or direct a group of two or more people to a desired outcome. In fact, we're all leading each other every day. We all have an influence on the people around us. What kind of influence depends on us.

Specifically, I'm talking about leadership opportunities on campus.

ASB—Associated Student Body

RA/RD—Resident Advisor, Resident Director

Organizational/club leadership

Class project leadership

Fundraising efforts leadership

Leadership is basically accepting responsibility for more than just yourself. It's learning to care for the success of others as well.

The thing to know about leadership is that it's not always easy. That's why there are so few leaders out there because, like Seth Godin said, "Few people are willing to go through the discomfort to lead." But what discomfort?

The discomfort of leadership is the fear of exponentially failing. It's one thing if you fail yourself, but if you're leading 10 people and you fail, the feeling, or fear of failing multiplies by 10—or more. Here's the great part: You are better than you think you are. And only when you are put into a leadership scenario where you have to sacrifice yourself and your own desires for the group do you learn how powerful and influential you can be.

If leading were easy, everyone would do it. Fortunately it's NOT easy, which means there are opportunities available. And not always, but often more perks, benefits, and pay are earned by the people in leadership. You know why? Because they deserve it.

A lot of people don't mind complaining about leaders, yet won't be courageous enough to step into that leader's shoes and see what they actually go through. The decisions they have to make. The negotiating they have to undertake. The time spent building and cultivating the relationships within the organization.

Sure, there are some leaders who let this power go to their head and treat the organization like a dictatorship. But that doesn't have to be you.

The world needs more leaders because we need more examples. So if you choose to take a leadership role on campus, you'll undergo the training and preparation necessary to influence people. It looks good on the resumé, but you'll also learn the true joy it is to positively influence people's lives.

When the opportunity arises, choose leadership. If you make that a habit, you'll find many more doors will open and your value in the marketplace will continue to rise.

---

## THE RIPPLE EFFECT OF MENTORS

### Julian Landry, University of Louisiana-Lafayette

At 16, I was arrested three times over a two-month period and was expelled from my small-town Catholic high school. Not exactly the kid people looked up to.

Fortunately, I found my first mentor when I was 18 through the sales company I worked for while I was in college. Before then, I was getting in a lot of trouble because I really had no direction in my life. I tried to get on the right path, but I couldn't seem to figure out how because I did not have any positive role models in my life.

I tried my hand in sales because I heard you could make good money, but I got more than I bargained for. When I was a brand new sales rep, I met a guy, Jordan, at a sales meeting. He was a student athlete at the college I was attending, and was very successful at the job. He seemed like an amazing guy, and I admired everything he accomplished. When I reached out to him, surprisingly, he was extremely willing to help, and I started to call him nearly every day.

Jordan answered all of my questions and was never agitated with my persistence in asking for help. He introduced me to people who also become mentors and positive role models. They had a major impact on, not just my job performance, but my life. I found that who you surround yourself with is who you become. Talking about becoming the best version of yourself was a foreign concept to me, yet it was so normal to these people. It was amazing to me that people like this even existed, and they lit a fire under me to improve in all areas of my life. By finding a positive mentor and role model to follow, I was introduced to the most positive circle of influence I had ever been around and had a burning desire to be my best self so I could give to others the same motivation, inspiration, and example my mentor gave me.

This has been my passion ever since. It was a drastic change from doing the bare minimum to get by that I had been doing ever since I could remember. I've been able to use my growth to give back and be a mentor, and I have helped other people be mentors to create a ripple effect of positive change.

If I could give one piece of advice to every college student, which I know could change their life forever and help them find true fulfillment, it would be to find a mentor or, better yet, find many mentors by surrounding yourself with the most positive, helpful, and inspiring group of people you can possibly find. Embark on the never-ending journey of becoming the best you that you can be because, in this process, you will find what you're passionate about. And once you find your passion, pursue it relentlessly, because that is where you will find true fulfillment and have more fun than you've ever had in your life.

# PART FIVE

# The Difference That Makes a Difference

# No Excuses

*What if Superman spent his time sitting at a bar,
being sad that he could be killed by kryptonite?
Do not let your limitations be your focus.
Have an abundant mindset and do what you can.*
—Joe Diaz

---

Invariably circumstances will arise that are incomprehensible to you right now. In fact, you may have already dealt with some things like this in your life. I had them, my roommate had them, and everyone will have something difficult happen to them in college.

There's no game plan for dealing with life-altering situations. The only thing that I've found that helps me is listening to stories of other people who went through challenging times, or made major mistakes, and how they dealt with them.

Life is real. Consequences are real. Here are a few stories of students who went through tough situations during college. Take note of the lessons they learned and how these situations empowered them.

In the moment it may seem impossible to make it through. Just remember, you may be on your own, but you are *not* alone. There are people on campus ready, willing, and able to help you, no matter what.

# DORMS
## Sasha Souder

It was my freshman year of college; I was 18 years old and taking my first step into living on my own and being independent. I was excited for the new chapter in my life and to meet new people. I never drank in high school, and I never gave into peer pressure. It was known that I did not drink and that I was the friend to call if anyone needed a ride home from a party.

Once I got to college, it was a whole new ball game. I have always been a social butterfly, and I have no problem meeting new people and striking up a conversation. I do not know why I felt that I needed acceptance from these new "friends," but I felt inclined to drink even though I did not want to or even care for the taste.

One night I was invited to go to this small party at the dorms. Since I did not like beer, I had someone get a fifth of vodka so I could get drunk faster and not have to drink as much. We started playing some drinking games, and everyone was playing with beer except for me. I was playing with straight vodka, drinking from the bottle. At one point during the game you had to "waterfall" your beverage until the person next to you stopped drinking theirs. So I started chugging the bottle while everyone was chanting "SAVAGE! SAVAGE! SAVAGE!" I felt awesome with everyone thinking I was so cool.

I ended up consuming almost the whole bottle with only three inches left within less than an hour. Since I had never drank in my life before, I had no idea how detrimental it could be. Next thing I remember is waking up the following morning in a hospital with an adult diaper on. I had no idea how I got there or why I was there. I was later informed that moments after I had chugged the vodka bottle, I had become incoherent with my eyes rolling in the back of my head, and I could not even keep my head up without someone holding it. They threw me in the shower to try and wake me up, but then called the ambulance once they realized I was still non-responsive. I was rushed to the hospital and was told I could have died had I not made it there in time. The alcohol had already gone far enough into my blood stream to where it was too late to pump my stomach. They had to pray that I made it out alive.

I had to pay the consequences by getting kicked out of the dorms, yet still having to pay as if I lived there. I was put on probation by the university, and had to go to an outpatient program to stay eligible to run cross-country for the school. Now that time has passed, I do not regret what I did; I learned a very valuable lesson and was able to turn it into a positive outcome. After the incident, I started focusing more on school and ended up getting a 4.0 GPA that semester. I realized how doing even one silly thing can change your life in seconds.

# RESILIENCE

## Sally Sagario, California State University, Long Beach

I was diagnosed with schizoaffective disorder at 16. Needless to say making it to college, let alone getting a degree, was remarkably challenging. An important aspect of being a student of anything is that there is going to be a point when a person has to graduate.

Unfortunately, a good chunk of my young adult life was on hold due to a lot of drama, mental illness, and the lack of will power. Not a great mixture.

I made it through most of my undergrad years without any major issues. I actually walked with my graduating class even though I still had to take five classes to complete my degree. I wanted to do that traditional cap and gown thing.

Then life got real. I found out I was pregnant. My boyfriend proposed to me. We had our baby. Shortly after that, I had my first psychotic break as an adult. Mental illness is no joke. It affected myself and my family. My fiancé broke off the engagement, and now I had a baby and still five classes to finish to earn my bachelor's degree.

This put me in a deep depression that would last months. After my third hospitalization, I was finally diagnosed with Bipolar disorder. Juggling my illness is something in and of itself, but then I had to finish college and take care of my daughters. It was a very dark and challenging time. I would try to attend classes only to drop them because I wasn't stable. There was one class I had taken and dropped so many times that the Dean of the school knew me because she signed so many of my waivers.

One day I saw a well-known advocate of mental health give a talk about her accomplishments while having a mental illness: at the time she was in review for her Ph.D. Her speech totally encouraged me to pursue a graduate degree.

That week I looked up colleges that would accept my very low GPA. I was enrolled in one of the biggest private schools in the country under provisional status. Resilience is defined as how quickly someone bounces back from failure. I'll be honest, I didn't bounce back very fast, but I did bounce back.

A few years later I graduated with both my undergraduate and Masters Degrees. Fortunately through my faith, the support of my family and church community, I made it. Hopefully my story reaches someone who might be struggling like me. You're not alone, and there are resources and people willing to help. You just have to take your life, exactly as it is, accept it and have faith that you can learn and grow out of any situation.

--------------------------------------------------

# THE GREATEST CHALLENGE
## Leanne Heng

I thought the worst day of my life was the day my boyfriend broke up with me. God, was I wrong. On May 9, the
week before finals, I woke up to my brother Harry calling.
He said one sentence that changed my life forever, "Daddy's
gone."

Everything after that was a blur. It didn't make any sense.
I'd talked to him the night before. He seemed happy! It didn't
seem like anything was wrong with him. *My dad wasn't gone?
It wasn't his time. He wasn't ready.* I wasn't ready. I was never
ready to lose my father, my partner in crime, my best friend.
I couldn't imagine my life without the most important man in
it.

At that point I had lived my life like most people do,
where they believe everything and everyone they have in life
is certain. For the rest of that day, I locked myself in my room,
and I kept replaying a voicemail he left for me the day I broke
up with my boyfriend of three years.

My dad said, "Leanna, it's not the end of the world. You're
smart enough, you're good enough to do it on your own.
Don't feel sorry about nothing. Listen to daddy. Daddy loves
you. It's not the end of the world."

He was my rock.

To top this off, right after finals I was about to take on a
summer management program at the company I worked for
at the time. How was I supposed to do that? How could I be
a leader, an example, a mentor to others when I had just lost
one of the most important people in my life?

My boss told me, "It's okay if you don't want to do this.
Everyone understands. We're here for you."

I thought to myself, *what would Dad say?* I knew it was
going to be difficult, but I knew I had to do it. I knew it was

my turn to continue my father's legacy and build a business like he had done.

That summer was extraordinary. I got to mentor a younger guy named Clay who had lost his mom almost the same time I lost my dad. Having the opportunity to share the qualities my father had with others meant everything to me. That year was the darkest most challenging year I've ever had in my life. Yet regardless of how much pain came from that year, I found so much strength. I learned the value of time and how precious it is.

I learned that you should never leave the house after an argument without resolving it and telling that person how much you love them. I learned the people you should have in your life are the people that are with you in your darkest times, not just when you're on top of the world. I learned that nothing will ever compare to the day I lost my father. I live life with more meaning and purpose because I understand that life is never certain.

## LEARNING THE LANGUAGE

### Alkhansa Siedahmed, California State University, Long Beach and University of California, Los Angeles

Five and a half years ago I moved from Sudan to Los Angeles with my family. It was a culture shock—everything was different from my country. I could not start college right away because I was not a California resident, and I could barely read, write, or speak English. I had to wait a year to establish residency, and during that time I started taking ESL (English as Second Language) classes at a local community college.

The classes were not really helpful because most of the students were Arabic speakers like me so most of the time I was talking to them in Arabic, not really practicing any English. I stopped going there: I had to find another way to teach myself English, but since I was not driving at that time, I could not go to any other places for ESL.

Then I started watching cartoons with my little brothers, and that was really helpful. I used to have a small notebook where I wrote words and vocabulary that I heard from cartoons, and at the end of the day, I translated and memorized them. Little by little I was able to understand English and speak a little bit. Then I was able to take my driving test. I started taking a few more ESL classes, and then I could take regular college courses.

It was so challenging for me to take classes like history, geography, and political science because I still did not fully get the language and was too embarrassed to ask for help. I used to take a dictionary to class to translate words. It was really frustrating, and I cried pretty much every day because I was stressed out about my accent and what people thought of me. Plus, I did not have any friends that could help me study.

I was missing a lot of assignments and didn't know when to turn them in because teachers were talking very fast and I could not understand. I passed that semester with 2.7 GPA. And at the point I knew that, in order to succeed, I needed to communicate with other people, students, and teachers, more effectively.

I took a sales job where I was forced to talk to people constantly, practicing my English. Being forced to talk with people pushed me to get over my fears. Fortunately, my coworkers took a liking to me and spent time teaching me idioms and slang I'd never learned in class.

That really helped me to improve my communication skills and gain confidence.

To me, academic success was not just about time management, staying on top of my assignments, or working hard. My college success was about learning to communicate effectively with teachers and classmates. Once I could do that, I started getting outstanding grades. I graduated from the Cal State Long Beach bio-medical engineering program. Now I attend medical school at UCLA.

---

# CHAPTER 26

# The Giver's Advantage

*Some people light up a room when they walk INTO it.*
*Some people light up a room when they walk OUT of it.*
—*Scott Greenberg*

---

An interesting challenge inside of college is that you can focus so much on you and your own growth and development that it's easy to forget about the other important things in life. Namely, the rest of the world.

I'm not saying you need to drop everything, join the Peace Corps, and move to a faraway land, although there are several summer, winter, or spring break volunteer opportunities out there to consider.

It's a proven fact that those who give are happier and more fulfilled than those who don't.

When we contribute, or do something that benefits others, we remind ourselves, T*he world is a better place because I'm here.* That emotion, or experience of believing that *you matter*, is the antidote for so many things that ail the human soul.

Depression is a huge issue, not just in college but everywhere. And since college is your proving ground to create the habits and skills that will equip you for the real world, learning to make unique contributions is *paramount* to happiness from the inside out.

Often when people experience depression, they are missing something. They haven't found a purpose for their life. It's not about what you have, it's about what you give.

It doesn't always have to be money. It could be time, energy and effort, or connections.

There are a lot of ways to give. Here's one I had the opportunity to spearhead on campus.

## ONE MAN'S TRASH IS ANOTHER MAN'S TREASURE

When I was an RA there was a requirement to host a project that was a contribution to the local community outside of campus. The idea just came to me.

At the end of every school year during finals week, I'd walk around campus and see dumpsters full of school supplies, books, pens, paper and the like. Students were traveling home and didn't want to bring the extra supplies they had accumulated through out the semester so they threw them away. Some things still brand new. It was such a waste.

There had to be some organization that would have great use of all these extra school supplies.

A month before finals, I started a used school supply drive and enrolled every dormitory on campus. There would be a box at the end of every hall, and during finals week, students were encouraged to put any new or new-ish supplies inside.

Every floor of every dorm had their own box, some filled up two or three. In the end we donated two truckloads of used school supplies to a local organization that supports after school programs and provides school supplies to students who couldn't otherwise afford them.

The man who picked up the supplies was so floored by our contribution.

It was so simple, yet so impactful. All it took was a little time and a little awareness. By the way, you can steal this idea and use it yourself. I believe every campus should do something like this every year.

There is no shortage of volunteer opportunities, just a shortage of willing volunteers. Find a way to impact your campus or community before you leave college. Whether you lead it, or are a part of it, the experience is worth more than if you were paid for it. You matter.

---

# AND A GOAT

## Jason Heinritz, University of Wisconsin Whitewater

What seemed like a small act of service turned into a ripple effect of goodness.

One of the ways I volunteered in college was to help my professor raise money to buy goats for families in Rwanda. She shared her passion about how a goat would help a poverty-stricken family and improve the health of the children through a site called *TheHungerSite.GreaterGood.com*. She was one of my favorite professors, and when she told me that raising only $40 would buy a goat and improve a family's life, I wanted to help.

She threw a challenge to the class to raise money for two weeks. We split into teams of two. My teammate and I decided to go for it. We were on the football team together and treated this mission as a competition. In order to win, we had to work harder and smarter.

We decided to get uncomfortable.

We went around the dorms asking people for change. There were 13 dorms we hit up. We went to each floor and knocked on each door. Only about a third of the residents were home and answered. We usually opened with a joke or something weird to get the conversation started. After sharing our teacher's passion and our mission, we asked them to give us any spare change to help the cause. Most of the reluctant students were convinced after we said, "You spent $5 in one night for a party cup. The least you can do is give something to troubled families in another country."

After two weeks of raising money in the dorms, we ended up racking up $480, and we were the top team in the class. Even though we were inspired by the competition and our teacher's passion, the mission carried beyond that class. Our actions inspired others in the class to raise more money and catch up to us. We even inspired other students to donate to their own cause. There was a newspaper article written up about the success of our team and the professor's mission.

In the end, we helped 12 families buy a goat in Rwanda. In the moment, we may not realize what our impact could be. What may seem like a small volunteer or service project could impact people forever. I will always be extremely proud of that effort. Find a cause that you believe in and spend some time devoted to it. You'll carry that joy and that sense of integrity with you for life.

---

## FIND A NEED, FILL A NEED, SERVE THE PEOPLE
### J. Brad Britton, Hardin Simmons University

What was that noise? As I walked out of the dorms, already late for class, there were fourth and fifth graders, hundreds of them, all over the small campus at my private Christian university in West Texas. I'd never seen or heard anything quite like it.

It was Western Heritage Rodeo Day at the university, and most of the fraternities, sororities, and many of the clubs and organizations on campus were sponsoring activities like knot tying, calf roping, and various arts and crafts. The kids were in smaller groups of 20–30 with one teacher trying to manage the kids and keep them together and focused.

As I strolled through the mayhem, I quickly noticed two groups of kids who were just sitting in the grass waiting for one of the stations to open up. It was obvious that the teacher was struggling to keep the kids from getting restless.

Well, I was already running late, and I'll admit that it didn't take much for me to find a reason to miss class altogether. So I made a quick trip to the drama department, where I had a good relationship with the person in charge of the costume room. I checked out a cowboy hat, a pair of boots, and a western shirt and some suspenders.

With a bow-legged walk and slow southern drawl, I meandered up to one of the groups that was sitting there doing nothing but waiting. Mustering up all the confidence and acting ability I could, I started to tell a story I'd made up about panning for gold out west and how a grizzly bear came up behind me, and how, with nothing but my trusty pocket knife, I wrestled with this wild animal and ended up with a bearskin rug.

It was rewarding to see how the teachers were so appreciative and relieved that the kids were entertained for a few minutes while they waited for the next station to open up. I spent a couple of hours going from group to group as my story got better and better. And then, as quickly as it started, it was all over.

About a month later, I kinda got in trouble with the administration (something about lighting fireworks in the dorms; it really wasn't my fault, honest), and as the conversation was at the toughest point for me, all of a sudden the college administrator, stopped, smiled and said, "You know, I saw what you did on Rodeo Day. It was really helpful, the kids loved it, and the teachers were extremely grateful. So let's just forget all about this little mishap and you do your best to stay out of trouble."

It's good to serve without expecting anything in return, but it is still nice when something positive comes back around.

# SEVEN WAYS YOU CAN MAKE THE WORLD A BETTER PLACE IN COLLEGE THAT DON'T COST YOU A DOLLAR:

1. **Give sincere compliments.** If you notice something special about a person on a certain day, make note of it in a genuine manner. You can be the source of someone else having a good day. Acknowledge someone for who they uniquely are. Practice becoming a finder of good in what other people do or say and you're sure to make their day.

2. **Smile more.** Try it out. Smile at people and notice what they do. They smile back.

    *The Smile Challenge.* Here's a crazy challenge someone gave me. Smile as big as you can into a mirror for 15 seconds then stop for 15 seconds. Then smile for 30 seconds and rest for 30 seconds. Then smile for a minute and rest for a minute. Then smile for two minutes and rest for two minutes. Keep going as long as you can. It's harder than you think, but I bet you'll learn to smile better because of it. I know I did.

3. **Listen.** By listening to people, we show them they are important. Taking the time to hear about someone's day or what someone is excited about makes them feel better. They feel like their words matter because they are worth listening too.

4. **Stop complaining.** Seriously, stop it. Ever notice when you tell a negative story of something that happened to you, the other person comes at you with, "Well, if you think that's bad, let me tell you about *this.*" Then you have a battle for who has the worst life. How do you feel after that conversation? Probably not excited to do anything good for the world.

    Oprah has a sign in her studio that says, "Pay attention to the energy you bring into this place."

Everyone needs time to vent, but if you find yourself venting more than you talk about the good things in your life, you might be bringing the wrong energy into the room.

5. **Don't gossip.** What you say about others says more about you than it does about them. Have you ever been on the negative end of someone talking about you? How did you find out? How did you feel? Whatever we do, we give others permission to do. When you gossip you're essentially saying that it's okay for others to do the same thing when you're not around.

6. **Help out the new guy/girl.** Can you remember being new somewhere? How did you feel about the first person who helped you out or showed you around? Those are the people we always remember. It's easy to get frustrated or annoyed when people don't know their way around, but remember, you were there, too. Lending a helping hand to the rookie just may pay off some day. At least you've got another fan in the world.

7. **Volunteer for upcoming events.** Some people think they should be paid for everything they do. The challenge is that when you don't have much experience, people don't offer you those positions. There will be so many volunteer opportunities that get you into free concerts and events and help you make friends you'd never have made otherwise. Surprise yourself and others. Do it for free!

# PART SIX

# The End
# of My Journey

# CHAPTER 28

# Redemption—
# The Last Chapter of
# My College Experience

*Listening for Inspiration*

I remember being told, "When the student is ready, the teacher appears." That moment came for me when I went to my first major sales conference for Cutco right before the summer of my senior year at Gonzaga University.

At the conference I met this guy named Hal Elrod, who inspired me to find something so passionate to work for that I'd be willing to put my whole heart in. That's the true way to overcome obstacles. Find a big enough reason.

But what did I care that much about? I'd already accomplished so much in previous summers, what else was there?

In the midst of all that I thought about my dad. He had now been living with Parkinson's disease for 4 years. Nothing noticeably changed for his first few years. Then one day while visiting home I attended church with my parents. I remember holding my dad's hand and feeling it involuntarily twitch over and over. The disease was real and it was here.

I thought, *What if I did something for my dad? How cool would it be to sell enough to make all the money I needed for school AND donate $1,000 to the Michael J. Fox Parkinson's Foundation?* So I put that idea into action.

Surprisingly, it wasn't as hard as I thought it would be. I told every client what I was up to, and they were in awe. I mean, how many 21-year-old kids are trying to pay for college on their own and donating $1,000 of their own money toward something that matters? Many clients even told me of stories in how they dealt with their own sick parents and it became this extraordinary bonding experience.

The experience changed me. By the end of that summer I cut the check for $1,000 to the Michael J. Fox Foundation. I thought the adventure was over but the best was yet to come.

## INSPIRATION INSPIRES INSPIRATION

At the end of the summer, my dad didn't know about the donation, although it was made in his name. The Michael J. Fox Foundation sent him the thank you letter. My dad called me, beside himself.

It was another one of those teary eyed, "I love you" conversations that mean so much to us, but then the phone was silent.

**Me:** Hello, are you there dad?

**Dad:** Yeah, I just have this idea. What if... What if I rode my bike up to your graduation from college?

**Me:** What... Dad... San Diego to Spokane, Washingon ... that's like fifteen hundred miles.

**Dad:** It's actually 1,830, I looked into it a little earlier...

If there's one thing I've learned in life, if someone tells you a dream, no matter how crazy it sounds, believe in them. It isn't always easy, especially when you know their track record.

Historically my dad was the one who'd say "Let's go to Disneyland" then bail last minute. So, I just kept those thoughts and comments to myself as we continued to talk about the journey.

Week after week, he'd give me progress reports. He hired a trainer. He created a work out plan. Mapping the trip out. Months and months went by, and I was just waiting for my dad to say, "You know what John, this just isn't realistic."

That call never came.

However, one month before the scheduled leave date for the trip, my parents had a problem... lodging. Where would they stay?

Stressed out, my parents decide to take a trip to Disneyland's California Adventure to get their mind off things. When they walked out of the park, my dad's phone rang. It's Doug, our paraplegic neighbor across the street.

**Doug:** Hey Ron, are you guys still planning on that bike ride of yours?

**Dad:** Of course, why do you ask?

**Doug:** Well, if you want some company, I could go with you, and we could take my RV so we all have somewhere to sleep. It just sounds like such a cool trip. I'd love to be a part of it.

**Dad:** *(fighting back his tears)* That... that would be great, Doug.

Prayers *do* get answered.

On March 6th, my dad left downtown San Diego on a 1,830 mile bike ride to Spokane, Washington for my graduation from college.

Let's not forget here that when he left, he'd had Parkinson's for over four years. Every day he had to take his drug cocktail in the morning then get on his bike for as long as he could before everything wore off.

My dad said the hardest part was when he couldn't control pushing one side of his body as much as the other side. You can imagine how scary that is when you are on back roads and giant semis blow past you.

On more than one occasion, he was blown off the road. One such instance, his bike cracked in half.

He called me that night, as excited as ever.

**Dad:** Guess what?

**Me:** What?

**Dad:** I got blown off the road, and my bike broke in half!

**Me:** What? That's awful.

**Dad:** No, it's pretty amazing actually. We went into town, and bought a new bike. I told them the story of our journey, so they rushed the bike to Trek. And they will have it fixed and delivered to Seattle for me to pick up in a month.

**Me:** *(grinning from ear to ear)* That's great, Dad.

That kind of thing happened almost too much to talk about.

One month in, averaging 40–60 miles a day, he crossed the California to Oregon border. He called to tell me the news. I was at a school retreat with about a hundred other Gonzaga students.

I put my dad on hold and shouted, "Hey everyone, my dad just crossed the midway point on the trip. Let's all show him how awesome he is."

I put him on speaker and everyone starts cheering and screaming. The phone went silent ...

**Me:** Dad, are you there?

**Dad:** Yeah, thanks John. I gotta go.

Later he told me that was one of the most extraordinary moments of his trip and he couldn't keep it together on the phone, so he needed to take a moment to weep. For him, it was one of those rare moments like when a professional sports team wins the national championship.

It was real. If he'd made it halfway, he could make it the rest of the way.

But he wasn't done. The last month every day was a miracle. Several times he just missed torrential downpours and snow.

We spoke nearly every day, which was more than we'd ever talked while living under the same roof!

On May 6th, various faculty, students, media and I stood in the quad of Gonzaga University awaiting my dad's arrival. My good friend Adam Sobieski said, "Dude, we need a finish line." He ran into the bathroom and grabbed a roll of toilet paper.

Then I saw him, my dad, wearing a yellow and black jacket. He rode into the quad at 3PM. He made it. He finished on the exact day at the exact time he'd declared he would. It may have taken three bikes, thirteen flat tires, and two months to get there, but he did it. It was a moment that defined something for me: Anyone can do something if they decide to do it.

Do you know what that lesson is worth to a child? Do you know how much this lesson has changed my life and the thousands who have heard the story?

Shortly after this experience, my dad's disease progressed rapidly. He had his chance. The opportunity arose for him to be courageous and he took it. He had every excuse in the book to sit back and let his sickness rule his life.

What's my excuse? What's your excuse? Whenever I think something is impossible, I remember this story and think, *Is it really not possible, or am I just not willing to do what it takes, to deal with the fear, to organize my priorities, to let go of other's opinions, or give up my vices?*

Most people don't take chances because of perceived limitations. Today, my dad has real limitations. He'll probably never be able to do something like that again. But that's okay because, when he could, he did. And now we have the story to share.

# GONZAGA

A QUARTERLY PUBLICATION OF GONZAGA UNIVERSITY

SUMMER 2005  VOL. 7  NO.1

# Dad bikes 1,800 miles for son's big day

*By Marcine Herron ('05)*

Ron Israel bicycled onto campus illuminated by the bright yellow jersey of a champion, and powered through a makeshift toilet-paper finish line. Awaiting him was his smiling, open-armed son John for whom Ron had cycled 1,843 miles from San Diego to see graduate.

For John Israel, his yellow-clad dad could have just won the Tour de France. Pride beamed from his face as he hugged his father before he dismounted his bike.

Ron's love-powered effort to reach his son's graduation was more than merely staggering; you see, Ron has Parkinson's disease. He averaged 35-40 miles each day of the two-month trek, fighting daily to maintain balance on the bike and straining to make his muscles answer his brain's commands.

Plans for the ride began late last fall when a son's passion inspired his dad.

At Gonzaga, John learned that it is better to be driven by passion than the desire for money and began to contemplate his passion.

"A little light flipped on," said John, a sales associate for Cutco Knives. "I would donate money from my sales to Parkinson's research. It just seemed logical." John worked hard enough last summer to meet his goal, and donated $1,000 to Parkinson's research in Ron's name.

Ron had wanted to start a foundation and, inspired by John, did so and then began planning the ride to raise $300,000 for Parkinson's research. He chose a scenic but difficult route following state Highway 1 and U.S. Highway 101 north along the California and Oregon coasts, then east to Spokane.

"I thought my dad was insane," said John. "It's 1,800 miles." However, Ron's passion and determination soon turned John's reservation to excitement.

John's relationship with his dad has strengthened since the Parkinson's diagnosis five years

*Ron Israel may have endured more than any other parent to make it to son John's graduation.*

ago. "Since the diagnosis, we have enjoyed an amazing connection," said John.

Likewise, Ron has inspired his son.

"He told me about this hill he was climbing during the trip that was taking every ounce of his energy and the Parkinson's was preventing him from having an even pedal stroke. But nothing would stop him," said John. "It made me think of the things I complain about, like 8 a.m. classes or studying instead of going out with friends. To have something you're truly passionate about makes these obstacles easy to overcome."

Reaching Spokane isn't the end of the story. Ron plans to continue the charity ride, hoping to show Parkinson's patients that a full, active life is possible. John plans to personally donate $2,000 every year until their $300,000 goal is met, and to promote his dad's rides.

"This won't be the last one, believe me," said John.

# CHAPTER 29

# It's Not About You

The challenge with college is that the requirements to succeed are so great and require so much attention, time, and focus that it's hard to stay motivated when it's all about you. What if the answer to a truly fulfilling college experience is *It's not about you?*

Zig Ziglar said, "You can have anything in life you want, if you just help enough people get what they want."

After reflecting on this quote, I saw the pieces of my college experience come together.

In the beginning it was about helping the skate companies I rode for to have a more successful business by promoting their brand and product everywhere I could, and they made sure I never paid for a skateboard again.

Then it was about supporting my university by creating a safe space for students as an RA, and in turn the university helped me live out my dream of graduating college by paying for my room and board.

That last year of college was the most rewarding of all, and you know what, it became about helping my dad live out his dream. It didn't matter that I wasn't the one in the spotlight because it felt amazing just to be a part of it.

When we shift the focus to serving others while we pursue our own goals, we access a deep well of purpose and resolve that isn't available when it's all about us. We find the fuel to endure anything and the end result is a more fulfilling experience.

# CHAPTER 30

# What About Skateboarding?

Invariably people want to know what ever happened with skateboarding. Well, I pursued it as far as my body would let me. A few years after graduation, my injuries tallied up enough to take me out for good. It was a good run though.

I traveled. I skated cool places, and signed autographs for people too young to realize I wasn't actually famous. It was remarkable. I'm grateful for having pursued it as long as I did. There's something special that forms internally when we pursue our passions as deeply as we can for as long as we can. We train ourselves to treat all aspects of life that way.

That drive has translated into everything I do now as a speaker, writer, and business person.

I hope you see now that skating through college isn't about finding the easy route. In fact, it's quite the opposite.

Skating through college is about discovering what you love and pursuing it with your whole heart and being willing to endure the pain, the struggle, the sleepless nights, broken hearts, failed projects, and embarrassing moments because it's part of the process. *We don't do it because we love the struggle, but because we love who we get to BE every day.*

# CHAPTER 31

# One Final Request

W hat you just read was advice from my own experiences in college and the experiences of dozens of other students from around the country just like you.

I hope it was of value and in some way, shape, or form makes these next several years of your college life easier than if you hadn't read this book.

Here's my one request: Write down 10 things you have learned from your own college experience that you would want to share with an incoming freshman.

You may have some answers now, you may not have some for a few months, you may even add to the list a year to two after graduation. Write them down on the rest of this page or in a notebook and share them. It could be a sibling, a cousin, or a friend's younger sister who's heading off to college for the first time. You can even send your ideas to me, and who knows, they might make it into my next book.

Make sure to stay in touch with me. I love hearing success stories from students via email or through various forms of social media. You can reach me on my website: *www.SkatingThroughCollege.com.*

I hope you have a blessed college experience and an extraordinary future as you pursue your passions and make a difference without sacrificing your GPA. If there is anything else I can do to add value to your life, please don't hesitate to reach out.

# MY TOP 10 LESSONS FROM COLLEGE:

1. _____

2. _____

3. _____

4. _____

5. _____

6. _____

7. _____

8. _____

9. _____

10. _____

# Acknowledgements

There are so many people I'd like to thank for in some way contributing to this book or who were a part of my journey of skating through college. If I forgot to include your name, I love you... please don't hate me.

First and foremost, I have to thank my parents, Ron and Kathleen Israel, for inspiring me to go to college even when it didn't make financial sense. Thank you for all the sacrifices you made for our family and me.

Thank you to all my siblings who supported me, let me sleep on your couch (Lisa), let me borrow your car (Carla), or fed me Thanksgiving dinner (Peter & Ceci).

Thank you to:

- Every person who influenced or impacted my skateboarding— Henry Daly, James Brockman, Jeremy Lebel, Chris Dobstaff, Adam Louder, David Dutton, Joe Utley, the Spirit Skateshop crew, Ted, Dave Schlossbach (wherever you are), Micah Shapiro, Marshall Reed, Kanten Russell, Laszlo Kellemen. All the companies who sponsored me or hooked me up with free product in college: LIB Technologies Skateboards, Nice Footwear, Tracker trucks, Aurora Wheels, Spirit Skateshop, Slick Willy's skatewax, Nova Skateshop.

- All the friends— leaders who were a part of my journey at Cutco or who encouraged me to finish this book. The San Diego crew— PJ Potter, Paul Comstock, Ron Geronimo, Adam Sobieski, Evan Keller, Dave Marson, Jesse Long, Candace Gomez, Josh Hall, Blair Berkely, Wes Goddard. Thanks for all the late nights, role-playing, and California Burritos.

- The Ventura team— Danny Ledezma, Brittany Smith, Perris Doucette, Spencer Dixon, Kyle McCormick, Jacob Sanchez, Chris Lee, Blake, Nandi Argent, and Sarah Tompkins. Thanks for being the best reps and managers I could have ever prayed for.

- My mentors and friends— J. Brad Britton, Aaron Love, Jon Berghoff, Hal Elrod, Jon Vroman, Dave Durand. Thanks for being the example I always sought to follow. Thanks for being the ones who paved the way.

- All the contributing authors who took the time to write and share their stories— Spencer Dixon, Kyle Murphy, Carey Smolenski, Megan, Peter Bieligus, BJ Ward, Nate Minkel, Erik Wilde, Michael C., Leah Recancia, Don Anque, Liam Kyle Cahill, Amiee Mueller, Michael Coscetta, Lena Z, Jamar Cobb-Denard, Julian Landry, Jason Heinritz, Sasha Souder, Sally Sagario, Leanne Heng, Alkhansa Siednamhamannidad, J. Brad Britton.

- Nicolas McCarthy-Moya...you are a big reason high school was a success for me. You showed me that it's possible to be smart, have fun, and skate at the same time. You were the best man at my wedding, and I still consider you my best friend.

I thank *you* the reader. For reading the whole book, even the acknowledgements. That's impressive. I mean, who does that? Thanks for giving me your time and brain space.

And, of course, my wife Monica. The best sports fans will root for their team when they are up by 10 or down by 20. Thank you for always being my biggest fan and support no matter what the score was. You're still the girl worth fighting dragons for.

---

# About the Author

J ohn Israel is a Nationally acclaimed speaker, trainer, and
author. His content has motivated and influenced tens of
thousands of college students across US and Canada. John
went from nearly dropping out of college for financial reasons,
to paying his own way, making $50,000 *during* his senior year,
and $100,000 his first year out of college. John holds a Bachelors
degree from Gonzaga University in WA state.

Made in the USA
Middletown, DE
14 July 2016